# PRAISE FOR

"A true story of survival, courage, faith, and a mother's hope and love for a child conceived by rape. Michelle's strength to move through her own shame and grief towards empowerment for the sake of her family is inspiring!" MD

"Michelle's determination and strength is evident in every line of her story. She endured terrible things and now lives with an unshakeable optimism that is an inspiration for everyone." ART

"This genuine and powerful story wrestles with tough topics, tougher decisions, and gut wrenching sacrifice. It's about choosing what will define you and finding strength and joy along the way. Only an amazing God could use harsh realities and challenges to create so much beauty. This story of love will truly warm your soul...it did for me!" KM

"Michelle's story is one of perseverance, love, and the redeeming power of God. Thank you for bravely sharing your story of redemption." LP

"Excellent read! Full of encouragement for life's tumultuous ups and downs. I love how the story evolved into an answered prayer of God weaving a dream to be a mother and reuniting with a child selflessly given up for adoption. As a fellow survivor of sexual abuse, I am thankful for the courage you have to share your story. It's definitely a road map for other journeys to forgiveness, healing, and restoration." GW

"Michelle's story is a testament to the power of God's faithfulness, timing, and redemption. A heartbreaking but timely story on the paths many women experience. I feel as though I know Michelle, and I loved learning how God redeemed her life through a devastating series of events in her adolescence." AE

"Through some of the darkest moments a young girl should never have to endure, Michelle tells her story of redemption, grace, and true bravery. In facing the pain of a secret too hard to share, she recounts a journey of betrayal and loss through which she found her voice and a warrior's will to fight. Even at 16, she knew that her journey would be bigger than herself. What she learned is something we all need reminding of - God is full of grace, unconditional love, and no man can ever take away the true joy that comes from Him." RT

"Michelle's empowering story of conceiving a child after rape will have you in tears. At just 16 years young, she experienced betrayal by people she trusted. She was ridiculed and shamed for her pregnancy, which had been through no fault of her own. Even in those dark moments, she kept her faith. With His grace, love, and mercy, she started her journey to healing and forgiveness." JM

"This is the raw and emotional story of a young woman's determination and real-life struggles. It is about trusting yourself, the process, and God. Ultimately, she was blessed with an overwhelming abundance of love, joy, and relationships, despite circumstance. The selfless decision exemplified in here resulted in Michelle being a pillar of strength for many with similar experiences. She has blessed my life tremendously and, for that, I am forever grateful. The emotions I felt were all over the place, tears of sadness and joy to say the least! I couldn't put the book down and finished it instead of sleeping! I give this book a 10 out of 10; I recommend it to everyone I know." SC

"I couldn't be more proud of Michelle for what she went through and accomplished. Undefined shows how something so devastating could be changed into something beautiful." JZ

"Michelle's is a story of how perseverance, strength, and unwavering faith got her through difficult challenges that no one should ever have to face. In spite of those challenges, Michelle became someone her daughter, and everyone, can look up to. Thank you, Michelle, for sharing your amazing story with the world." SH

"I could not stop reading this book. My emotions were touched in so many ways, from shock, anger, disappointment and sadness, to feeling the elation of Michelle's joy, happiness, forgiveness, and healing. The unfailing hope she carried is a testimony to God's faithfulness." JC

""You don't ever need to let others decide who you are. You get to choose who you will be." To define something is to give meaning, shape, and clarity. A person cannot be defined since they are made up of the moments, events, emotions, and how they respond. It's a process, a lifelong journey. Michelle's is a journey through her moments that have not defined her deep capacity for love and joy in the face of dark and heart shattering moments. The way Michelle so transparently bares her soul and tells her story is simply beautiful." KA

""You still have fifteen minutes" … I will never forget those haunting words that began a spiral of pain, guilt, fear, and shame in Michelle's journey. However, I quickly learned that she refused to let rape or betrayal define her, but rather fell into a deep, unwavering love for her daughter. Leading a life of grace and triumph; a true overcomer!" JB

"In this book, Michelle tells a gripping and very personal story of her journey of faith in God through some incredibly difficult circumstances. She is honest about her own mistakes, as well as how others misguided and let her down, but she does so in a gracious and forgiving way. This book reveals the story of a young woman's journey through incredible pain, as well as her choice not to allow that series of events lead her into a life of bitterness, but rather one of joy and productivity. Definitely a book worth reading and one that I will recommend to others." CG

"This story is so full of hope, love, and, most of all, the goodness of God. It's very empowering to see that turning this tragedy into triumph could only have been done with God's love and perseverance. I was able to relate to all the characters and felt like I was reading about family. I highly recommend this book to all; whether you have been affected by rape or adoption in any way, this book will restore your faith in God." JJ

"While this book has a strong message of both faith and motherhood, it is so much more. I want everyone I know to read this book. It is a message about resilience and determination. I want to know more about Michelle, her life, and her family." JN

# Undefined

*More Than the Sum of my Losses*

Michelle Lee Graham

This book is dedicated to Sarah Kay Syms.
You single-handedly defined my life!

# TABLE OF CONTENTS

# ACKNOWLEDGEMENTS

## FAMILY

Adam Christopher Graham

Thank you for your love and support when I had to follow my dream to write this book. For stepping in to make dinner, pick up the kids, turn down the background noises, and give me time and space for my journey. Thank you for your love and dedication to me and our beautiful family.

Sarah Kay Syms

Thank you for allowing me to share our story. For being open to giving me insights and encouragement. I love that you were willing to share your perspective. We jumped into this relationship hoping for something special... we have been given more than we ever could have imagined.

Daniel Scott Ross

Thank you for giving me the great privilege of becoming a parent. From your conception, you have inspired me to be a better person. The years, together and apart, have made me the mom that I am proud to be today. I pray that your dreams stay big and I am honored to call you my son.

Jacob Nicholas Ross

I greatly admire your strength and independence. You are not afraid to take risks and you are willing to work hard to get what you want. Your loyalty and quiet steadfast behavior is honorable. I miss the boy you were, but love and respect the man you have become.

Rachel Michelle Ross

It is hard to find words that can express how much I love you, how important you are in my life, and how much I cherish every moment. You have brought me a life filled with happiness, friendship, and fulfillment. I love you Dippy Lippy!

Lauren Elizabeth Hart Graham

My Sweet Girl, I love you so much. Thank you for doing your best to be patient as I wrote this book. For knowing that it was important and giving me the time to pursue this dream. You inspire me with your love for life and zealousness. Your humor and wit bring our family so much joy. You are compassionate and strong, everything a great leader is.

Mason Christopher Graham

I prayed for you to come into my life and am thankful every day for that answered prayer. You bring our home so much laughter. Your brave and outgoing personality shines so brightly. You inspire me to think outside the box, in creative and unique ways. I love you with my whole heart!

Cathie Monroe

Mama, I love you with all of my heart. Thank you for your love and support throughout my lifetime. I cherish our special memories and always look forward to more. Your belief in me has been consistent and I have always known your love. Your forgiveness for others is nothing short of a miracle. People often ask how I was able to forgive so deeply. I know; it was the example you set throughout my life.

Larry Monroe (RIP)

Dad, thank you for showing me how to be loved. For setting the expectation high for any other man to fulfill. Thank you for always being proud of me and supporting my decisions even when they hurt. I miss you every single day and I always will. Until we can dance again…I love you Dad!

John Monroe
I cherish the life we have shared together. Through childhood, you were my brother, best friend and playmate. As an adult, you have been a rock I can lean on. You are an amazing husband, father, son, and brother. I knew our lives would always stay connected. Now, with so many miles of physical separation, my heart only holds you closer.

Yukara Monroe
Thank you for the years of listening to me as I lived out this journey. For asking me questions that made me reflect and dig deep. Thank you for believing in me along the way. I am grateful to have a sister-in-law who I consider such a close friend.

Tom Syms
Thank you for accepting me wholeheartedly. Your welcoming smile and gentle laugh always brightens my day. Your deep thoughts and perspectives demonstrate your character and strength. I am thankful for the man you are for Sarah, a godly husband who is faithful to his family. Thank you for welcoming me into your life with open arms.

Khrystina Elizabeth Ross
Thank you for joining our family in such a special way. Having you as my daughter-in-law has brought me so much joy. I have prayed for you your whole life, knowing that God would bring Daniel a beautiful, godly woman to live his life with. Though you have just arrived into our lives, you have been in our hearts a lifetime already.

Aunt Jennifer

I am so grateful for having grown up with you. You have always taken your role as my aunt very seriously, since the mature age of eight, when I was born. Thank you for stepping in so many times when I needed a helping hand. Your generosity is never an expectation. Thank you for showing your love when I needed you most. You've always been there for me, to listen, cry, celebrate and rejoice. I love you with all of my heart.

Donna Lynch

I am grateful that we were able to share our own stories of adoption; a unique bond that we alone share. Having somebody so close, who understood my pain, brought me immense healing. I love you my aunt, and thank you, for all you have imparted into my life.

Dorothy Monroe

Grandma, how do I find the words to express how much you mean to me? You have taught me so many lessons, both about our family and about life. You encouraged me to go to college, even when it seemed an overwhelming feat. You inspired me to look past societal norms and follow my dreams. You shared your wisdom…your secrets are forever safe with me.

Barb Neal

I didn't know it would be possible to open my heart again. However, you showed me that it was safe. You welcomed me and my children with open "Gramma" arms. Your charisma and zealousness for life helps me feel it too. I admire your love for others and willingness to give people a chance. Your life demonstrates forgiveness, healing, and an inner strength I greatly value.

## FRIENDS

Alia Escalante

Your friendship means the world to me, as I'm sure you already know. I cherish our childhood, and young adulthood, for the memories that we share. My greatest joy has come from our relationship now. You know me, love me, and see my heart. Though our visits are few and far between, I look forward to them all year. We've never outgrown Magic Money and sleep-overs.

Celia Kibler

Your new friendship came at such a special moment in my life. A time when it felt like all was lost in my book endeavor, you were the value I gained. Thank you for your advice, friendship, and shoulder. Hugs to you, my friend.

Charlene Sousa

Childhood friendship, special and true. You have been, and will always be, the person I can run into and pick up exactly where we left off. Thank you for being a part of my journey in life. I love you dearly, my friend.

Jacqui Banta

Though God has brought me many people over the years, many who have come and gone, you have remained. The past three years have brought me a friendship that I didn't even know I needed. You came into my life at exactly the perfect time. We have learned with each other, from each other, and by trying it together. I am forever thankful that God brought you to my life, yours is a friendship I will cherish always.

Jeff & Marie

You impacted my life in ways that I cannot even express. I am forever thankful. I hope this book brings new insight and answers. I will be forever grateful for our special bond.

Jennifer Jamison

When our worlds collided, we could not have been less prepared. The loss of losing our parents would bring us together, but time and mutual love would keep us here. You are, and will forever be, the most important gift at the time of my greatest loss. Thank you for your forever friendship.

Jill Copeland

Thank you for a friendship that has withstood the test of time. For more than two decades, we have been blended into each other's life. Sometimes intentionally, other times by happenstance. Each time, drawing our friendship closer. Thank you for your sincerity and love.

JJ Vercellono

I thank God for bringing you into my life at the perfect time. I enjoyed the memories that we made together. Although only for a short time, they will stay with me for a lifetime.

Karen Gularte

How do I put into words how much your friendship means to me? For more than 30 years, we have created memories, shared our lives and been uniquely intertwined together. Although you were not named directly in my book, you were certainly one who God gave me to help me heal and live a life full of joy. You have always been willing to listen as I shared stories of my pain. You let me vent when I needed to express frustration and doubts. You were there to celebrate all of my wins. I am thankful to be Auntie Michelle to Megan and Jason. I love you, John, and the kids. Forever!

Kerri Mallory

Thank you for your years of friendship. Through the troubled times, you did not give up. I have always looked up to you, for affirmation and approval. Your life over the years would prove I was right. You are a beautiful example of a wife, mother, and grandmother. I have admired you up close and from afar. You are precious and special in my life.

Kimberly La Belle

I would like to express my complete gratitude. You have been an integral part of my journey. Your willingness to hear God's voice and share His promises has been a true blessing over the years. I am forever grateful for your steadfast faithfulness to Christ.

Mike Jamison

Thank you for opening up your family and home to welcome mine. With outstretched arms you have made us feel like family. Thank you for investing your time and your love into our lives. Family Nights will always be my favorite night of the week.

Nurse Patty

You have been my angel on earth. Sent at the perfect time, imparting me with love, wisdom, and a better understanding of the world. You are a true example of thoughtfulness and gentleness. I will forever be grateful.

Sarah Coffey

I am thankful that God gave us each other a unique story that we alone get to share. Your encouragement over the years inspired me to hold on to hope. Watching you grow up, from a young child to the beautiful woman you are today, blessed me beyond belief. Knowing that I was watching another birth mom's daughter grow into a woman made me feel honored and privileged in ways that I could not even fully understand.

Tim & Sharon (RIP)

Thank you both for the words of encouragement you imparted to me. For teaching me how to take care of my young pregnant body, preparing my meals, and insisting I take my prenatal vitamins, even when I just threw them up. Thank you for your gentle support. Tim, your faithfulness to your family was a true example of what a good man is.

William Hoffman

For a decade, you have been my mentor and partner. You have taught me to be a better CEO, daughter, parent, and friend. Thank you for all the wisdom you have imparted and the jokes you have shared. Thank you for encouraging me when I came up with this crazy idea to write an entire book. Your impact on my life will last forever.

Students at Allan Hancock College

I wanted to give a shout-out to my Allan Hancock College students. You first inspired me to tell my story. Your questions and curiosity helped inspire me to write this book.

## MAKING OF THE BOOK

Writer & Editor: Alexa Tanen

I cannot thank you enough for helping make my dream come true. You were able to help me organize my thoughts, simplify complicated issues, and help make my writing succinct and beautiful. You added defining words, flow, and were able to capture my tone. You helped me ensure that the reader could truly hear my heart. You knew this was important to me and helped me to get to this beautiful end result. We come with such different perspectives and yet you were able to help me stay true to mine. You listened and truly heard me. I will forever be grateful.

Coach: Emee Vida Estacio

Thank you for your guidance and leadership. You stepped in when I needed direction and helped put the important things into perspective. Thank you.

Editor: Abbey Espinoza

Thank you for your edits and review. Your feedback was appreciated and provided an opportunity to go even deeper into my story.

Cover Art: Justin Cappon

Thank you for making my story visually come to life. You listened to my hopes and dreams and made them beautifully appear on my cover.

Photographer: Stephanie Adkisson, Distinctive Images

For 20 years you have been my personal photographer. Family photos, senior pictures, and, of course, my wedding. This opportunity was likely the most special of all. Photographing Sarah and me when we reconnected, as you know, was my dream come true. Thank you for capturing the moments.

Formatter & Artist: Rocio Monroy

Thank you for the beautiful formatting and artwork that you added to my book. Your creativity, professionalism and expertise helped make everything come together perfectly

Book Reviewers:

Thank you to all who were gracious enough to read my book ahead of time. Your feedback, insight, reviews and guidance was heard. Your thoughts, both positive and negative, helped make what it has become.

# INTRODUCTION

## *Undefined*

This is not a sad story. This is a story about holding on to hope in the face of overwhelming tragedy, of learning how to forgive and not let the trauma define me, of learning to trust God to bring me through. This is a story about turning that tragedy into triumph.

Growing up in a close, Christian household, my life was happy and full of love. My brother, only eighteen months my junior, my mom, and my dad all lived together. I was always an outgoing child. I was the first to rush in to tell everyone about my day and demanded endless attention from our parents. My brother, John, on the other hand, was more quiet (though whether by nature or necessity, I don't know). He was the friend I could take with me throughout life. Our weeks were simple, but we had an established routine. In addition to daily school activities, Sunday was for church, Tuesday was family night, and Wednesday was for church youth group.

Socially, I had many friends, both at church and school. I looked forward to life, each day, and was easily pleased with the little things. Family night was one of my favorites. Mom would make a delicious meal and, after dishes, Dad led us in a family bible study. After that, Dad, John, and I would climb into the car to head over to a local arcade. Neither Dad nor I needed many coins because we'd always beat our own high score from the week prior. A dollar or two gave us plenty of game time. John ran around from machine to machine, racking up tickets and quickly spending his allocation of quarters. Once he was out, he began his regular hunt for other people's coins that had inadvertently rolled under a machine or been dropped in a corner. These were memories I'd cherish my whole life.

My family always gave me everything they could and I was content knowing they tried their best. We had modest means; my father was a car mechanic and my mother was a preschool director. Though sometimes they couldn't give me everything I wanted, I was never left in need.

I've never resented God for the events that happened. The people who betrayed my trust or the decision my parents felt they had to make in the face of unimaginable circumstances. While traumatic in ways I will never be able to forget, those events made me who I am today. I discovered not only my strength of will, but also a great gift in the midst of heartbreak.

# ONE

# *Undefined by Rape*

*"And God shall wipe away all tears from their eyes; and there shall be no more death, neither sorrow, nor crying, neither shall there be any more pain: for the former things are passed away." (Revelation 21:4)*

The year I was sixteen, my faith was truly tested in a way I could never have imagined. Like many teens, I decided to have an after-school job. A little extra pocket change for new clothes wasn't nearly as enticing as the personal freedom and responsibility afforded by it. I'd been looking for a way to prove to myself and my parents that I could be trusted with having a car after I'd lost their trust the year prior. As a freshman, I'd had an older, more experienced boyfriend for a few months. We'd ended up being intimate, despite my religious convictions. The guilt of that transgression still weighed heavily upon my shoulders. In light of that, my parents had allowed me to have a car with the caveat that I could only use it to go to school, work, and church. I was determined to show them that I deserved this second chance.

I began working at a local fast food restaurant. A few weeks in, I was confident in the new environment and had met most of the staff I regularly worked with. One night, I met a manager for the first time. I hadn't seen him around before, but he explained it away by reminding me that I was still new there. He was in his thirties and had likely been working at the chain for some time. We hardly spoke and I didn't think much of him during the shift other than to note that the other employees found him congenial.

This particular night, I was working a closing shift. When we'd finished cleaning and locking up, I followed everyone else out to the parking lot. The new manager was already out there, unsuccessfully trying to start his motorcycle. One of the other employees called out:

"Oh hey, you okay?"

"Yeah, yeah. I'm fine. I'm fine."

He continued to fiddle with the ignition, frowning as he did so. I'd always been raised to be polite.

"Is your motorcycle not starting?"

"No, I'll be fine. I'll be fine."

Shrugging nonchalantly, I made my way to my car. Just as I began to get inside, my mind already halfway home, he approached me. His voice was hassled, verging on annoyed.

"Well, now that you mention it, I really can't get this thing started. Would it be cool? I live just right up the road. Give me a ride?"

I was torn. Here I was, desperate to keep my promise to my parents about my driving, having only been working for a couple of weeks. It was the end of a long shift, very late at night. I couldn't stop thinking about the last time I'd broken their rules and been caught in sin. However, the Bible teaches that we should help those in need and, more than that, my father had always made time to pull over on the road to help people with vehicular troubles.

I may not have had his mechanical expertise, but a short ride down the road was something I could offer and it seemed like the right thing to do. I knew my parents would understand, approve even, and making a good impression on my boss couldn't hurt. I cleared my throat, decision made.

"Well, where do you live?"

"About a mile from here, just up the road."

He gestured in that direction. I bit my lip, thinking of the time.

"Okay, because I actually need to get home. My parents are watching the clock."

Even if I hadn't disobeyed them before, it was still late into the evening, and I didn't want to worry them.

"Oh, yeah, yeah. No, you'll be right home."

He reassured me quickly and abandoned his motorcycle, climbing into my passenger seat. The drive itself was short, as promised, and nothing seemed amiss. We made idle chit-chat as I drove. He thanked me again for giving me a ride, commented that he enjoyed working with me, and was sorry he hadn't seen me around before. None of the traditional alarm bells went off in his company. He was well-spoken, casual, and quite friendly. Growing up, I'd been taught to be on the lookout for creeps and violent guys, but I wasn't prepared for a predator to be charming, to put me at ease. He continued to disarm me with compliments, while keeping the focus on work.

"Wow, you really worked hard tonight and you're going to go far. And you're really charismatic. You've got a great personality, great customer service, and people really enjoy working and connecting with you."

I appreciated the praise, thinking that a manager must know what he's talking about. A few minutes up the main road, he let me know we had arrived and I could feel free to drop him off. Despite the flattering conversation, I was relieved. I wasn't very far from my house and didn't think it would take long enough to get back that anyone would be worried. I quickly pulled over, not bothering to put it into park, and waited for him to hop out.

"All right, see you next time!"

"Yeah, for sure. I'll see you next time," he paused momentarily. "But I really don't want you to leave yet."

A sense of uncertainty bloomed but, not wanting to be rude, I rapidly said: "Oh no, I have to go! I've gotta go! My parents are going to be waiting for me."

"Well, you got off work early. It was only 9:45 when we left. Your parents are expecting you by what? 10:10? 10:15?"

The fact that he was so keen to know when I was expected back home left a dry taste in my mouth. Little bolts of adrenaline zipped up and down my spine; my heart pounded. I didn't know why, but I needed to get away. Urgently. I half-chuckled nervously.

"Oh yeah. No later than 10:15 for sure."

"Well, you still have fifteen minutes."

I began to stumble over my words, the anxiety ratcheting up my throat.

"N-no! I have got to go! I have to get going!"

He continued to insist I still had time to stay, but I mustered my courage and blurted out: "I'm feeling uncomfortable!"

I'd never felt pressured before the way I experienced that night. The nervous jitters made my arms and legs shiver. Fight or flight instincts had fully kicked in by then, and I felt more and more sure that I needed to leave. It was glaringly obvious that he had sexual motives in mind, but the entire scenario was ridiculously far removed from anything I could have envisioned. He was an unattractive man in his thirties and I was a teenager. Legally, still a child!

"You know, I'm a supervisor. A lot of the girls at work have been really attracted to me, but I have to push them away because I'm too old for them. You're way more mature."

His tone was meant to be reassuring. I listened in disbelief as he went on to discuss his own proclivities and the hordes of women he supposedly had fought off. Disgusted, I barely heard his actual words. Finally, I firmly told him to get out of my car.

"Oh no, no. Don't be a prude. I'm not trying to do anything with you. I just enjoyed your conversation. You were so friendly. What happened to your vibe? You were smiling earlier. What happened to you? What's going on?"

I tried to insist that he was making me uncomfortable. Instead of listening, he started to argue, wanting to engage me further and make me feel guilty for my discomfort. Years later, I'd know that this is a classic predatory tactic, but at the time, I would have agreed to anything, said anything, just to make him leave.

"Well, what makes you uncomfortable? I'm not even touching you. What if—I mean—would it make you more uncomfortable if I touched you?"

As he spoke, he reached out for the first time and laid his hand on my leg, skimming it quickly up the inside of my thigh. I shivered in revulsion and reiterated:

"You need to stop! Please, leave! Get out of my car!"

"I'll leave in a minute. Remember, you have fifteen minutes." He paused and corrected himself to my everlasting horror: "actually, I have fifteen minutes."

Terror coursed through my body. My heart raced faster, my palms sweating. If I'd had any doubts about what was going to happen, they'd been erased with those words, and I was left floundering. Time seemed to slow, or maybe my thoughts sped up. Did I smile too much? Did I say something I shouldn't have? How did he get the impression that I wanted this? Was I flirting? Leading him on? In my panic, everything boiled down to: is this my fault?

My gut sank. The guilt began to eat away at me before anything had even happened. I knew what he would do. Worse, I remembered how my mom had reacted when I revealed my past indiscretion. How could I do that to her again? I felt as though I was losing consciousness from the terror, like I was outside of myself as it happened. Later, I'd learn the words for an out-of-body experience, but then, I wanted to be just about anywhere else but there. I tried hard to project my consciousness out and away. It wasn't completely effective. The searing brands of his hands yanking down my stretchy work pants. The hot press of his heavy body holding me down, the awkward angle making it impossible to fight back. Almost worse than the physical sensation were the words he spoke, continuous and rambling, punctuated by gasping inhales.

"You want it so bad. You want this. You're begging for it. You're going to love this. This is what you've been wanting. All night you've been looking at me, telling me you wanted it with your eyes. Now you're going to get it."

I kept telling him "No, I don't want it. I have to leave. My parents will be upset; they were probably already worried about me. They'll come out to find me."

I felt it when my foot slipped off of the clutch. The engine sputtered and died, along with any hope I might've still had that I could escape. Abruptly, he grabbed the handle of my chair and it fell back. I began crying in earnest, pleading with him.

"Please, don't rape me. Please, don't rape me!"

He only answered that it wasn't rape because I wanted it.

"I don't! I don't want this! Please! Don't rape me!"

When he tired of hearing my pleas, he covered my mouth so tightly I could barely breathe. He murmured over and over that it would hurt less if I relaxed. My body was wound taut; I couldn't have relaxed even if I'd wanted to. Is this how I would die?

I remembered hearing stories of other girls who had been raped, the ones who lived and the ones who didn't. I'd led a relatively sheltered life, but it was impossible to not have known or seen items in the news. I repeated to myself: as long as I live through this, it's okay. I just have to live through this.

My legs were shaking with fear and tension. Fleetingly, I wondered if I could fight back—how could I fight back? Do I kick him where it hurts? Can I maneuver that way? Are my legs flexible enough? Should I scratch his face? Tear and claw at him? Would a punch be better, maybe shove him away from me enough to breathe? Should I bite his hand? Will he let go? If only I could take a breath, clear my head, have a moment to think, just get him off of me, get him off!

But no matter how many jumbled thoughts of protecting myself rapidly swirled around my brain, I couldn't move. I was frozen in fear and pain. I laid there, trembling, concentrating on trying to get air through his meaty fingers where they clamped over my face. The tears and snot poured down my face and I gasped for breath. His slick hand could only dampen the sounds of my sobs and they echoed in my ears, intermingled with his panting. I imagined a thousand ways I could hurt him, how sensitive his eyes would be to my nails, how he'd groan if I kneed or bit him. The pain was severe, but the panic was all encompassing. I remembered the stories. I remembered what parents taught their children.

Times have changed in the intervening decades. We encourage women to be alert, attend self-defense classes, to be loud and resist when not faced with a lethal weapon. We now know how cowardly rapists truly are. Back then, though, we told our daughters to submit. If I didn't submit, I might not live through it. Just give the attacker what he wants, and he'll leave you alone. The most important thing is staying alive, and you have to do anything to stay alive. I thought it would be safer to succumb than face his reaction. Who knows what might have happened? That unknown ultimately frightened me more than the rough treatment, than the degradation he spewed, or the assault itself.

Soon, but not soon enough, the worst was over. He had gotten what he wanted. He released my mouth and I desperately pulled the stale, heated air into my heaving lungs, my heart still rabbiting in my chest. He glared down at me and snarled.

"Pull your pants up, you slut!"

I hurried to comply, fumbling for my pants where they'd become twisted around my ankles. My entire lower half throbbed in agony. Eyes still wet with tears, I looked up at my attacker and, in that moment, I believed him. I was a slut, and this whole thing was my fault. The looming terror of what would happen next barely held the shame at bay. I waited while he tidied himself up, hoping against hope that it was over now. He won't hurt me anymore; he won't kill me or kidnap me. I gave him what he wanted; I didn't fight him.

Thankfully, he hauled himself out of the car without a word, slammed the door, and never looked back. All he left was the musty smell of sweat and grease, stinking up my car. The need to flee surged through my veins once more and I drove half a block, desperate to put distance between me and that dark shadow before he changed his mind and came back for me.

Then, everything hit me. I pulled over and bawled. I cried for so many things that night, soaked in that disgusting odor, permeating every thought I had. The shame finally overwhelmed my fear and I wallowed in the term "slut," applying it to myself to justify what had happened. The guilt was suffocating; how would I ever tell my family? My hysterical cries slowed as I thought about my parents. I couldn't let them know what had happened and my fifteen minutes were long expended. They'd undoubtedly be worried.

I scrubbed at my face with my work shirt, a rough polyester thing, to wipe away any evidence I'd been crying. The mascara that'd run down my cheeks, the snot on my lip, the tear tracks, it all needed to be erased. I couldn't do anything about swollen and red eyes, though, so I brainstormed excuses as I made my way home in case my mom noticed. I readied a couple of scenarios, all revolving around events at school, normal things that might make a high schooler cry, but when I pulled up, I saw that all of the lights were out inside. I knew everyone had already gone to sleep. My relief was indescribable.

I could just go inside, take a shower, and pretend none of this had happened. It had all simply been a bad dream. I'll wake up tomorrow and no one will have to know. The door creaked as I slowly pushed it open. I stepped quietly on to the carpet, terrified suddenly that someone was hiding in the shadows; that they'd take one look at me and know that I'd been raped. If anyone saw me, they would know. The vulnerability of the night made me feel transparent and I crossed my fingers that no one would look. Softly, I announced my homecoming, but no one answered.

I locked the front door and went straight to the bathroom. I didn't bother bringing fresh clothes, towels, nothing. I couldn't stand the thought that every second I wasn't safe and alone in the shower, anyone could wake up and come see me. See what had happened to me. See what kind of slut I was. I ripped my work clothes off, thinking if I could get his stink off of me, I could rid myself of his touch entirely. Before I could get in the shower, I caught sight of myself in the mirror. I had a moment of contemplation. I viciously began to ask this girl, this naked, vulnerable girl, the questions I'd been too afraid to face.

Who are you? How did this happen to you? What did you do to get here? How are you here? And then, when she didn't answer me, my thoughts turned to the future. How would I live with this? I'd made so sure to stay alive, but that was worth nothing if I couldn't figure out how to go on. Did I have to tell anyone? After a minute of staring, I shook my head. No. Only he and I know what happened; I don't have to tell. No one else has to know. I let the scalding water wash away my tears and all traces of the night, determined to bear my shame alone. I had to be quiet, lest I wake the household up, but I couldn't stop crying. My shoulders shook and my knees gave out, letting me down hard against the porcelain. I snatched a hand towel from nearby and began to scream into it, desperate to muffle the noise.

Amidst my grief and despair was anger too. Where was God in all of this? Why hadn't He intervened, stopped this from happening? What had I done to not deserve His protection? Hadn't I been faithful enough? Hadn't I repented my sins? I knew in my heart that I had not. Part of me suspected that this was my punishment, that God intended me to bear the weight of that night because I'd broken my vows and lost my virginity the year before. Despite that, I still cried out to Him. Could this punishment truly fit my crime? All my life, I'd believed in Him, reached out to Him to love and protect me. Even knowing what I'd done, how could He allow this to happen?

When I realized I'd get no answers, I finally noticed that I'd lost track of time and the water had gone cold. With no towel, I used a washcloth to dry myself. I wrapped myself in my mother's pink bathrobe and rushed to my room, still intent on not being seen. By the time I'd put on clean pajamas and climbed into bed, I was exhausted enough that I'd come to terms with God's lack of intervention, knowing in my heart that He was with me and that I'd need Him, more than ever, in the coming days.

Bizarrely, I managed to get some sleep that night. When I awoke, the sun was out, and I felt refreshed. I tried to convince myself that I'd imagined the events of the past night. That, as long as I laid still and quiet in bed, I could still be the girl I was yesterday; the girl who hadn't been raped. My mom stuck her head in.

"Good morning!"

I managed a half-smile. Something in my head clicked: she couldn't see it. My mom, who had known and loved me for my whole life, couldn't tell what had happened just by looking at me. And if she didn't know, no one else would either. A spark of happiness swelled in my chest. I could keep this secret! No one would have to know after all. I could keep my pain to myself, and my parents wouldn't have to bear it alongside me. My whole life, my mom had been hyper-aware of my activities to prevent just such a tragedy from happening. She had always taught me to keep my wits about me and had worried when I spent time at friends' houses when their fathers or older brothers would be home. She knew what could happen to a growing young lady and she desperately wanted to keep me safe, as all parents do, but expressly about rape.

When she left again to go about her morning routine, I continued to lay there, watching the sun rise through the fog. I knew then that life goes on. No matter what had happened to me or how dark it had been the previous night, the sun rose once again. I knew it would rise the next day and the day after that. I took solace in its constancy, knowing that I could do that too.

Rising myself, my body immediately made me aware of the assault through various aches and pains. There would be no denying it to myself, not when it was so fresh. Sweatpants and a cozy sweater made it a little more bearable, but not by much. I tried to think about the sun and the new day ahead of me, projecting as much confidence as possible. Eating breakfast with my family, I almost believed nothing had happened at all. But it wasn't easy.

Things would occur at random, shattering the normalcy I tried to surround myself with. A simple word, "slut," said carelessly from my television. Someone becoming angry enough to display violence, no matter where it was directed. Even something as simple as overhearing "Hey, your car broke down? Let me give you a ride!" These events would trigger me and suddenly I'd be back in my car, my manager on top of me again, the terror shooting through me. My legs would tremble and my palms would sweat. Everything I wanted to suppress came rushing back.

In the back of my mind, I knew what that meant. I knew I couldn't spend the rest of my life re-experiencing that trauma, and I needed some kind of help. But help would only come about if I told someone I'd been raped, and I was still determined not to do so. I really hoped that a combination of faith and sheer strength of will would be enough to conquer it. I couldn't bring that kind of shame and hurt on my family, especially not my mom. I knew it would truly devastate her to know the truth and I just wasn't prepared to do that.

When the time finally came, many weeks later, for me to tell someone, I started with my two closest friends. I was terrified of revealing this secret; I had no idea how they'd react. Would they dismiss it as no big deal because I'd already had sex before? Would they ask me why I didn't fight back? What would I even say to that? Why didn't I fight back? Would they even believe me? Much like before, I had no answers.

The catalyst was realizing that I had missed my period. At sixteen, I was old enough to know what that could mean. Until that moment, it had never occurred to me that the rape could result in pregnancy. Logically, I knew that any sex could lead to becoming pregnant, but I'd been so focused on containing the event to those fateful fifteen minutes, and then had been so happy that it was finally over, that I'd never imagined anything else would happen. This was what shattered my ability to pretend it hadn't happened. I'd been slowly managing to convince myself over the past few weeks that it was simply a vivid nightmare, but this was an unshakeable reality I couldn't do anything about.

Whatever worries I had about questions I couldn't answer, I had to tell someone. I couldn't handle this on my own. I needed to talk. Luckily, my friends were very supportive. They believed me, when I could hardly believe myself. One of my friends, Kerri, passionately pleaded with me to involve the authorities, hoping that I'd be able to have him arrested and get justice for myself. Maybe even get closure. My other friend, Alia, took another route, encouraging me to get counseling. Both of them made sure I knew I wouldn't have to face this on my own.

# TWO

# *Undefined by Betrayal*

*"It is better to trust in the LORD than to put confidence in man."*
*(Psalm 118:8)*

O nce I had explained the events of that night to them and been comforted, I had to tell them the most pressing issue: the reason I'd finally come forward about the rape. I had missed my period. Neither of them imagined that I could possibly be pregnant. They insisted that it was merely late or the schedule had been thrown off due to the immensely traumatic stress I was under. I wanted to believe them, so I agreed and accepted their answers. I wasn't sure, after all.

But if I was pregnant, why couldn't it have been Jason's baby? I did care for him while we dated, very deeply, and I still felt that affection a year later. In a moment of weakness, I called him. He was surprised to hear from me, but it was immediately clear that he still had feelings for me as well.

I missed him. I told him I wanted to meet up, and he agreed. We ended up being intimate once more, and it felt like I had regained some of the control I'd lost in the rape. Jason gave me back some of that confidence and the powerful knowledge that I was desirable. I could still be sexy, no matter what had happened. He couldn't tell what that man had done just by looking at me. I wanted to be the one in control of my body and my decisions, not anyone else. Also, I could now tell myself that the baby could be Jason's. At least there was a chance, no matter how fleeting. I tried to focus on my friends' words, though; it was probably nothing.

However, a couple weeks later, when I still had not started my period, I realized I needed to buy a pregnancy test. I knew it would be difficult, but I couldn't keep living without knowing one way or another. I went to the local pharmacy with some money I had been saving the past few weeks as a precautionary measure. At the time, an average pregnancy test cost about $15 minimum. I walked over to the Family Planning aisle and moved down to the section with pregnancy tests. It felt like tons of eyes were boring into my back, watching my every move. Surely everyone in the store was staring at me. Judging me. Sneering when I wasn't looking. A flush of humiliation crawled up my neck and my face felt hot. I wanted to die.

"I don't remember what my mom said she wanted?"

I raised my voice unnecessarily, practically shouting through a hoarse throat, desperate to satisfy those judging eyes, those scathing accusations they were surely leveling at me. A stupid teenager who got herself pregnant. In hindsight, I'm sure no one paid the slightest bit of attention to me. But, just as I was starting to consider simply melting into the floor in shame, I forced myself to focus on the task at hand. And was promptly overwhelmed by my options. I had no idea which type to buy! Some were pink, some were blue, some had words like "Yes" or "No," and others had lines or plus and minus symbols. I felt a little sick just looking at all of them. My entire future was in a six-inch cardboard box. Which one though?

I ended up going to the counter with a few different tests, hoping the cashier would be able to give me some useful advice or information. The woman gave me a shrewd look and the transparency from before suddenly came rushing back. She asked,

"Is this for you?"

It'd never been in my nature to be a liar,

"Uh, well, I'm buying it."

In the end, I didn't have enough money to buy the test I'd wanted, so I bought what I could afford: the cheapest test they had. I felt like somehow it made me cheap buying that one, and I wanted to melt into the floor again. After handing over the money, the cashier winked at me and said:

"Good luck."

Undoubtedly, she meant it in an offhand way. As I walked out of the store, those words swirled around my mind, both as whispers and a deafening roar. Good luck. Good luck? What did she mean by good luck? Does it mean I should be pregnant? Does it mean I hope I'm not pregnant? What the hell is good luck? Over and over I wondered, for the rest of the day. It was such a strange send-off, I hardly knew what to make of it.

Robotically, I threw away the receipt and the box, making sure to carefully save the instructions, and got into my car. The same car that held the memories I'd tried so hard to forget. The car where I might have been impregnated. And, if I had been, would that change my memories of the event? Would rape take on a different significance if I knew now what else would result from it? I wasn't ready to face those ideas. It had to be one step at a time. Violently shaking my head, I hid the test and its instructions as best I could and went to call Alia.

"I need to take this pregnancy test, but I don't want to take it at home."

Alia immediately agreed to let me come over and spend the night. No hesitation, no interruption to ask her parents for permission, just complete acceptance and support. I will always be grateful for how thoroughly she was there for me. I went to her house for the sleepover, and we tried to be as normal as possible. We caught each other up on the everyday things, joked around over sweet snacks, and went for a walk. She'd picked up on how much I wanted to be a teenager again and tried her best to distract me, but when we went out walking, it all came crashing down. Suddenly, a thought entered my mind: I wonder if today is the last time my life will ever be the same?

As we walked down the road, my senses were heightened. I could hear the cars whizzing past periodically as the loose gravel crunched under my feet. The scent of freshly mowed grass filled the crisp air that spring night and I'd never felt so alive. That moment has been etched in my mind. Would it be the beginning of something life-changing? Something too profound for me to fully comprehend? Or would this end up being just another day in the life for a high school sophomore? Which option did I even want anymore?

Alia knew me so well—since junior high. We shared school, church, youth group, and more than anyone else, she understood where I was coming from. We'd always tried to spend time together, but ever since her mom remarried, our visits were few and far between. The distance wasn't enough to dampen our friendship though. It was the first time in a while that I would be spending the night, and it was with ulterior motives that drove us together. We wouldn't be giggling about cute boys or gossiping about the cruelties of popular girls. I saw her look back at me from where she'd walked ahead, waiting for me. She asked if I was coming, but I knew what she was really asking: Are you okay?

"I'm here."

It didn't answer her question, but I didn't have an answer for her. I just wanted her to know how much I appreciated her presence, her unflinching support in the face of such adversity. How much closer I was to okay by having her there with me.

Despite that, myriad emotions flowed through my veins. Nervous, excited, scared. They slipped through my fingers, fleeting, while I did my best to hold on. My heart in my mouth, Alia and I read the instructions for the test again and again. One line was negative, two lines were positive. It all seems so simple in retrospect—a yes or no question. Did you or didn't you? Are you or are you not? Yet, this supposedly simple question bore so much more weight than any I'd ever asked myself. The answer could change my life. I still refused to accept the possibility. It wouldn't be true, couldn't be true. It was only at this point that we realized that the instructions for the test said it was most effective when taken first thing in the morning. Frustration overcame us briefly. I couldn't even find out that night? I had to wait until the morning? I gritted my teeth and bowed my head. It wasn't very late and we had a lifetime to wait.

That night, like many sleepovers before, I had laid, cuddled up with Alia in her bed. We could hear her parents moving around throughout the house.

"Do you think they know? That I came here to take a test? That I might be pregnant?"

"I don't know…"

It's funny to look back at childhood, how I always assumed that parents knew everything going on.

"What happens tomorrow? What if it's yes? What do I do?"

"Then you're going to have a baby, and I'll do anything I can to help. You can make this work, you know. You're the most capable person I know, Michelle; if anyone can do this, you can."

"Yeah. Yeah, okay. It won't be easy to tell my parents, but I believe you. I'm in, okay, I'm in."

I swallowed the sob lodged in my throat and tried to calm my breathing.

"I hope it's negative, but if not, maybe I'll be okay. I just don't know."

Otherwise, we were a pair of sheltered, good Christian girls. We weren't used to lying and keeping secrets like this from our parents. Finally, finally, the sun rose once more and morning came. Alia shook me awake; I didn't realize I'd ever fallen asleep.

"It's time! It's time! Let's go!"

Alia sat cross-legged on her blue bathroom rug and I crouched over the porcelain. My shaking fingers fumbled over the foil. Alia had the creased instruction sheet, folding and unfolding it again as she prepared to walk me through the process. To make sure I could tell the difference between one line or two. We had to do this right. But I was about to pee, right in front of her! Gross! I took a deep breath.

"Okay-"

"Wait! Try to pee on the spongy part."

"I have to go now!"

"Just aim a little!"

"What if I pee too soon? I can't hold it any longer!"

"It's okay, it's okay. Just relax and hold it right up there. You can't miss."

"Okay, here goes."

I squatted over the bowl and began the laborious process of aiming the stream of urine over the tiny head of the stick. The stick that held the secrets of the rest of my life. I managed, just barely. The instructions said we had to wait another three to five minutes for the results to show up on the stick. We sat with baited breath, our eyes glued to the small window. The first line appeared and I gasped, clutching Alia's hand hard enough to bruise. A second line materialized. My head began to pound as I frantically searched my memory: what did two lines mean again? Alia had reached for the instructions once more, her eyes scanning the text. I mumbled the same phrase I'd rehearsed all morning.

"One line is no, two lines is yes, one line is no, two lines is yes."

The words meant nothing as they fell from my lips. I heard them and yet, they did not register. I raised my voice slightly to capture Alia's attention again.

"Two lines is yes."

A wave of pride washed over me at unraveling the mystery, but it was quickly followed by us both realizing at the same time what that actually meant. A moment of silence hung in the air as we stared at each other.

"F@$%"

I'd never heard her say anything so vulgar before or since. It was so out of character—the ridiculousness of the situation was too much. The release of tension bubbled out of us in a bout of uncontrollable, semi-hysterical laughter. Nothing about the revelation was funny, but the expletive and unbearable weight of the situation begat only giggling. Giggling like the little girls we were. Like our friendship was a precious commodity, and it wouldn't be threatened by my changing fate. Like the loneliness wasn't lurking on the edges of our time together. That I wouldn't be forced to tell my parents. All of the secrets I'd been carrying, mostly on my own, for seven weeks would have to be exposed.

I had been using those secrets for strength at times. No one else knew what had happened and I could be myself. I could behave like no life-changing event had occurred. I was still the same me I'd been before. I was so good at hiding it that I could start to believe I wasn't lying at all. Maybe I still was me. But I knew the truth: something had happened. I had changed. I hardly recognized my own reflection anymore. Who was this girl who lied so easily to the people who loved her? Who held secrets so tightly that they changed her and pretended to be someone else?

Back in the cold bathroom, I started trying to process the situation. Alia did her best to cheer me up as we started getting ready for the day, even managing to find a bit of excitement. We didn't know any better.

"Just think about it! You could be a mom!"

"Well, I have always wanted to be a mom. Not now, not while I'm still a kid myself. But it's been a dream of mine. Maybe this isn't the end of the world. Maybe this isn't the worst day ever!"

We had no comprehension of the hardships involved in motherhood, the sacrifices a mom has to be prepared to make. I wasn't ready at sixteen to take on those challenges, but I had no way of knowing that yet. It was a knowledge that would take time to dawn on me. At that moment, it was one bright thing in an otherwise overwhelmingly devastated situation. I had to hold on to that.

"We should call Kerri and tell her."

I knew she'd be anxious to hear the news. We'd be seeing her soon in church, since it was a Sunday. We called her anyway, careful to speak vaguely on the subject so none of the other people in the house would know what we were talking about. Kerri was shocked and seemed unconvinced. She kept asking questions that neither Alia nor I had the answers to. We finally had to hang up and assured her we'd discuss the details once we saw her.

The second we saw her, Kerri rushed up to us asking what happened.

"The test was positive, and Alia cursed!"

Everyone burst out laughing again. The fact that Alia had cursed seemed almost more important than the actual pregnancy. Or maybe it was too hard for us to comprehend, so we focused on the part we understood. We managed to pull ourselves together to go into the church and head over to sit with the youth group. The pastor began the lesson and asked us if anyone had a favorite song. The three of us quietly began singing "Papa Don't Preach" by Madonna. It was completely unplanned and it sent us into gales of muffled laughter again at the spontaneity. As long as we were in church, together, I could cling to innocence. It wasn't until it was over and I knew I had to tell my parents that the laughter of the morning finally faded completely.

I knew my time was up; I had neither the desire nor the ability to keep the secret any longer. Despite that, I was terrified to tell my mother I'd been raped. No matter how I presented the tale, she'd blame herself. Feel that she'd failed to keep me safe. Protecting her meant more to me than the relief of exposing it. She already knew about my previous relationship with Jason, my ex-boyfriend, and how we'd gone "all the way." I reasoned, at the time, that it would be far easier for her not to know the circumstances of my pregnancy beyond the basics. I gathered my parents together after church and announced that I had engaged in sexual intercourse and believed I was pregnant from the encounter.

"What? With who? Jason?"

My mother was the first to break the bewildered silence. I winced internally and hedged.

"No, someone else."

They both stared at me, incredulously. I suddenly felt a spike of fear that I might not be believed. My heart thudded in my chest and I nearly opened my mouth to tell the full truth of the matter, but I had resolved not to and I couldn't break that. I took a deep breath instead. My mom had already been put through learning I'd had consensual sex the year prior and she'd been able to accept it and move on. She would surely not be able to do the same with the knowledge of my rape.

"How could this happen?"

I just shook my head and looked away, unable to meet their eyes while still hiding things from them. I felt so ashamed. My father, who had always been my world, my everything, who I'd trusted to have my back, then said something I couldn't wrap my mind around.

"We never should've moved to this city."

It was so random and seemingly off-topic that it threw me off. I gazed at him blankly, wondering what he could possibly be talking about. We'd lived there for most of my life; it was undoubtedly my home. More than anywhere else, at least. It's obvious now that people's minds make strange connections in times of grief and shock. The need to assign blame somewhere for random happenstance is very strong in humans and it gives us some strength in trying events, no matter how unconnected the object of blame is. Before I'd had time to respond, he followed it up with:

"You'll have to give the baby up for adoption."

Suddenly, I deflated. Only an hour before, Alia and Kerri had reassured me that I could be a good mother. We'd fantasized together about this bundle of joy I'd bring into the world and how I would raise the baby.

There I stood, the father I trusted more than anyone else, telling me that I resolutely could not do that, and I'd have to give my baby away. I had no choice but to believe him. He was my protector. I'd been raised to believe that he knew what was best for me and had no reason to mistrust that now. My father was very smart; he'd been right in the past and most of me knew that he was equally right at that moment. But a small part of me, the feisty part, wanted to rebel—still thought that I would be a good mother anyway. It hurt to hear him keep bringing up adoption as the only option in this situation and, for the first time in my life, I truly considered arguing with them, or trying to disobey.

In the end, I decided it was fine. I could just focus on getting through the day. Everything else was a problem for the future me. Just get through today. Nod and say yes to everything they're saying. Agree now and we can face what comes when it comes. But I still wondered: could I be a mom? Why couldn't I? I knew I was a good person, nurturing and kind. Now that I'd had some time to process the shock, I was a little excited to be pregnant. That day, I assumed that I'd done the hardest part by confessing to my parents. I figured that if I could make it through that, I could conquer anything. On top of everything else, I couldn't face the fact that I'd already taken the pregnancy test and knew for sure. They were still talking like it was a hypothetical scenario, and I wasn't ready to explain my secretive testing.

My mom went to the pharmacy and bought another pregnancy test. The guilt nearly choked me, remembering how expensive those tests were. We hardly had enough money to spend on necessities and here was my mom, spending it on frivolities I could have told them I didn't need. But I was too much of a coward to stop her. I tried saying that I'd pay her back for the test, but she waved me off. She clearly didn't care about spending the money; she saw this as a necessity, and she would have done anything to make sure her daughter could know for sure if she was about to face the biggest challenge in her life.

She left, right there and then, to purchase the test and have me take it. I thought about telling her how the instructions specified it needed to be taken first thing in the morning, but there was no way to do so without revealing my previous experience. I swallowed down the words and acquiesced. I figured it wouldn't matter; I knew in my heart that I was pregnant and I expected the test to reflect that. Somehow, though, it didn't. It came back negative. My mother was so relieved. She hugged and congratulated me. I wanted to be enthusiastic too, to smile sincerely back at her and really believe it. But I didn't. I knew I was pregnant. I don't know why I was so strongly convinced, but I was, and I could only return her hugs half-heartedly.

"We'll see, Mom. I have still missed my period for several weeks, so I think I need another, better test. We'll see, okay?"

"We'll have to take you to the doctor, of course. Just to make sure there isn't anything wrong."

I agreed. It may not have been confirmed yet, but the moment I heard Alia curse, the pregnancy was completely real to me. In the days leading up to the doctor's visit, my parents were on edge. It wasn't long before the doctor finally confirmed what I had known the whole time.

My mom made the appointment and brought me to the doctor's office, but she didn't stay throughout the examination. I guess she thought it might be embarrassing for me, or that I would be more open with the doctor without her in the room. The first part of the appointment consisted of me peeing in a cup for them to conduct the pregnancy test. It was easier than aiming onto the end of a small stick, but somehow more disgusting. I could feel the warm liquid in the cup, spilling over onto my fingers and I winced. Once I'd delivered it and the cup was sent to the lab, the second part of the exam began.

49

The doctor wanted to physically examine me to make sure I was healthy enough to sustain a pregnancy. I didn't want to discuss the rape and just demurred when asked about the specifics of why I thought I might be pregnant. Despite my resistance to bringing it up, it was all I could think about. I changed into a hospital gown and put my feet into the stirrups, hardly prepared for how violating just a basic exam could be. A full pelvic exam, complete with swabs, was both painful and humiliating on a good day. But, when my thoughts were full of a man taking advantage of me, every movement, every touch was electric. Each one shocked me and I couldn't help but jerk, trying to move away from the doctor's fingers every time. She gave me a sympathetic look and cooed to me, like I was a little kid, but her words fell on deaf ears.

When the lab tests came back positive, she questioned me again about when the intercourse took place. When I told her, she estimated the due date and my heart immediately sank. My legs felt watery and I couldn't stand up for a moment. Without knowing it, she'd said my own birthday. My baby was due to be born on my seventeenth birthday. Anxiety, far worse than any I'd ever known before, made my vision swim. I was still processing the fact that I was carrying another person inside of me, but, for some reason, the knowledge that the person would also share my birthday felt like one step farther. It was honestly exciting! That my child and I could also share a day of birth; one more aspect for us to have in common. It was all a lot to wrap my head around and my parents took the news much worse.

In the days that followed, an air of depression permeated our home. Every time I walked into the kitchen, my mom had puffy eyes, like she'd just been crying. My dad would leave a room when he saw me, swallowing down his own emotions. I couldn't mention anything about the pregnancy because no one wanted to hear such dire news. I felt guilty for every shred of excitement because it was obvious that no one shared those feelings. It became increasingly difficult to regulate my emotions about being a mother.

While I was still a little girl. I was their little girl and they didn't want me to be a mom. But it wasn't anything that any of us could change. I was pregnant.

I kept coming back to my original question: could I be a mom myself? If not, then why? I'd heard of girls my age having babies and being able to be good moms. If they could do it, surely I could as well? I knew I was resourceful; I'd proved as much before. But I couldn't even talk it out with my family, whose opinions I valued so highly. They were stuck on adoption and any alternative was simply out of the question.

Days went by and the safe refuge where I had hidden away from the world had transformed into something foreign. It was no longer my home, but a prison I longed to escape. School, church; I was willing to go anywhere as long as I wasn't there. The sadness was suffocating and I was responsible. A permanent pall fell over our household, and I knew I was to blame. It was painful how much grief my very presence brought every time I entered a room. I needed to leave.

Spring came to a close and summer neared, bringing with it the promise of freedom from school for most. For me, it brought dread as I contemplated having no reason to be gone most hours of the day. Yet, there was a hope on the horizon. For months, our church youth group had been planning a three-week trip to Washington, DC. It was contingent on us raising the money, but the trip had been important to me, even before the disaster of pregnancy had been forced upon me. I had been running myself ragged with fundraisers for months to raise the money. Car washes, selling candy, barbeques, every kind of hustling imaginable. My friends weren't quite as supportive as I'd hoped, telling me I wouldn't be able to go in light of the pregnancy, but I didn't see why not. They could hardly understand; I needed to go.

However, I had another hurdle to face. Neither my parents nor I had yet told the church about my pregnancy. My mom explained that the chaperones would need to know I was pregnant on the trip since I would start showing during that time. Plus, if I needed medical attention, they'd need to know what to tell the doctors. Surprisingly, I had no qualms about telling people. Even through everything, I was still excited and wanted to be able to share the news with others. Not that I could say that to my mom. Nor could I tell her that I'd started coming to terms with everything lately; I had really started thinking that I could really be okay. That I could do this. And I had started to truly love the baby growing inside of me. I knew everyone would eventually find out anyway, when I got large and wasn't able to hide it anymore. I thought that I could find joy in telling people about the beautiful little boy or girl I was carrying.

Being the one to tell people, before they found out otherwise, also restored a sense of control over the situation. A control I thought I'd all but lost during the rape. But allowing this pregnancy was within my control—the child's fate was within my control, and the choice between adoption and parenting was mine as well. I knew my mom was sorry I had to tell the church because it was a sad thing for her, and I did sympathize to some extent, but not completely. I couldn't tell her about the joyful part of knowing I'd be a mom; she wasn't there yet. Maybe she never would be.

This isn't to say I was healed of any anxiety. I was plagued by uncertainty and fear. I had time to think about it, but I still had no idea what I wanted to do. I knew how important transparency was to the church since my mother worked there. She'd been wanting to come clean, and I consented. The pastor was immensely disappointed to find out and informed us that, in order to be allowed on the DC trip, regardless of money I had raised, I would be required to tell the entire youth group that I was pregnant and to apologize for my indiscretions. I didn't understand the significance of that, but I resigned myself to doing as he asked. The trip was too important to me.

Before I could carry out such an apology, I was at a youth night function. Several friends around my age were also there to watch movies. Altogether, there were about eight of us. One of them was the pastor's son, who I'd known for most of my life. His father had apparently told him about my pregnancy already. He commented to me at one point that he'd heard.

"Yeah, I am. I don't know what I'm going to do yet, though."

He frowned at me.

"Oh, my parents said you were gonna put your baby up for adoption. I mean, we know a really good agency. It's the one we got my sister from. They said they already connected you with the agency."

It really bothered me that people were talking behind my back about something that would be my choice. A choice I hadn't even made yet. Here was this kid rambling about an adoption plan, concerning my baby and my life, and I hadn't even been invited to the conversation? I clenched my fist and tried not to take out my frustrations on him.

"All right. Thanks for the information. I don't know what I'm going to do yet, except start telling people. I haven't really told many people and there are a few I'd like to hear it from me."

I told him about his father's ultimatum and how I'd decided to tell the youth group about the pregnancy in order to be allowed on the DC trip. But before that, I wanted to privately tell a couple of people. He nodded and, apparently having finished with our conversation, turned back to the group at large to announce:

"Hey, let's do a soda run! Who wants to go?"

Everyone knew he'd be the driver. There were seven other people, including me. I wasn't about to try and cram myself in the car with everyone else.

"I'm not going. Does anyone else want to stay back with me?"

The youth leader, a man in his mid-thirties who I'd known for years, said he would stay back and set up the movies. I knew they'd only be gone about ten minutes and still didn't feel like going, so I decided to stay with him and assist in setting up. Not long after they left, he began making small talk.

"So, how are things going with you?"

"Well, actually, I'm kind of glad we have a few minutes to talk without everyone around. My mom already talked to the senior pastor, but I wanted to talk to you. Just to let you know that I'm, uh, I'm pregnant."

I didn't know how else to say it, and I didn't want to beat around the bush with him.

"Wait, what? What are you talking about? You're pregnant?"

"Yeah, it wasn't willing or anything…"

I tried to be vague.

"But it happened and it's over. And I'm okay. But I'm pregnant. So, anyways, I'm going to start telling people about it. Pastor wants me to tell the youth group before the DC trip."

"Well, wait. No, I want you to slow down, way down. I want some more details. What happened? Who did this?"

It felt protective, like he was gearing himself up to go find this man and kick his ass. It was nice, having someone who cared in that way.

"Is it someone I know? Someone in the church? Is it one of our youth? Are they here tonight?"

He started getting fired up and the warm glow from the protectiveness faded. I just wanted him to calm down and get back to setting up.

"No, it was just this work thing. And I don't know who it was."

I continued to be as vague as possible, unwilling to part with details if he was going to keep pressing me like that.

"I just really want to know."

"I don't know. I don't want to get into it. I don't even remember most of it; I've blocked a lot of it out."

"Let me see. Let's walk you through it. You were where? Where did it happen?"

"It was in my car. I had given someone a ride home."

"All right, so you're in your car. What's the first thing he did?"

"He put his hand on my leg."

"Oh, like this?"

He put his hand on my leg in a strange parody of the night I was remembering. I stuttered out some kind of affirmation, the touch sparking a sudden onslaught of anxiety. I laughed awkwardly, waiting for him to take it away. He left his hand where it was. I cleared my throat.

"Yeah, like that. So, it happened, but I'm fine now. I'm moving on, but I wanted you to know that I'm pregnant. Since I'll have to tell everyone soon."

"No! I need more details. Then what did he do? Is this what he did?"

He unbuckled his belt and unzipped his pants, leaning over me, pressing me down.

"Please don't!"

I cringed in horror, deflating completely. I had no fight left. The fear both for my own well-being was now combined with fear for the baby growing inside of me. If I resisted, would he hurt me? Hurt my baby? Be overly rough with me? Rough enough to possibly cause a miscarriage? I didn't know what kinds of things he could do, had never known he was capable of rape, much less anything else.

I also didn't know what types of activities would be harmful so early in the pregnancy. It wasn't some stranger I'd just met, he was a youth leader I knew and trusted. I told myself to just go to a different place mentally. I allowed myself to close my eyes and disassociate from that moment into another world. My body shifted and writhed in the warm sand of a beach, under the powerful rays of a hot sun. I listened to the waves crest and crash gently against the surf, trying to match my breathing to them.

Everything happened so fast. In the midst of my beach, I remembered to relax. Relax so it won't hurt as much. Just relax because it hurt so badly the first time. I couldn't stand that kind of harm again, not when there was so much more. Not when a life besides mine was at stake. At one point, in my mind, I vividly remember hearing words from the first time, in that manager's whispered growls, telling me again and again to relax.

At that moment, I changed. All trust for authority, leadership, people who claimed to be godly...trust in the world as I had known it was gone. It would take years to heal and I knew I had been changed. It was just moments. As quickly as it began, it was over.

"Is that what happened? Is that what he did to you? I'm so sorry that happened to you."

He literally flipped the script; like we were still continuing our conversation from before. I stared at him, incredulously. I thought he was absolutely insane. He kept talking like nothing had happened, like the past few minutes never existed and I was the crazy one for thinking they had. Even as I watched him wipe himself off and readjust his clothes, he jabbered away, totally normal. Unable to stand being around such a psychopath any longer, I hurried away to the bathroom and melted onto the floor. Just then, everyone returned from the soda run, and I had to muffle my cries.

How could I be so naive? How am I so trusting that I allowed myself to be in the exact same situation, only a couple months later? I felt so incredibly weak. That anyone could trample over me in every way conceivable. They could just take everything from me. I felt defiled, raped in a way that was somehow worse than the first time. This time, my religion had hurt me. My trust in humans was gone, obliterated with that violation. The very leadership who I thought were there to support me betrayed my trust.

This sense of being raw took over. I retreated into myself, unwilling to either trust others or allow myself to feel. I'd seen what kind of damage those expectations had done to me and a numbness was all I had left. It took me years of hard work to regain the person I wanted to be. The girl I was before so much was taken away from me. Sadly, I knew then that the actual physical abuse was the easiest part to move on from. The loss of control, of choice, of respect were all more permanent. Being transformed into a piece of meat and forced to be someone you're not, both during and after.

The effects were long lasting. When I was eventually able to be in healthy, consensual relationships, I couldn't stand being told how to feel. The second they did that, I became defensive. When people say there's no reason to be upset, or I should be happy about something, I just snap back at them: you don't get to do that. You can't take away my agency, not now, not ever again. Those men took it from me and I'll never fully erase that loss. The youth leader took more from me, I think. The manager was a near stranger, but I had spent so long looking to the youth leader for spiritual guidance and protection. He spat in the face of my trust and the God he claimed to be devoted to. Despite all of that, I had survived two separate incidents. I was still alive. I had a child who needed me and I was determined to keep going for them.

# THREE

# *Undefined by the Church*

*"For all have sinned and fall short of the glory of God..."*
*(Romans 3:23)*

I was practically desperate at that point to get away for a while. The situation at home was only more tense since I had withdrawn into myself, and I couldn't bear the shame of trying to explain to my parents that a leader from the church they loved and trusted so much had violated me when I came to him in confidence.

I couldn't wait for the DC trip. For three weeks, I could forget about the pregnancy, the rapes, and just be a kid again, seeing the East Coast. But, before I could do anything like that, I needed to follow through on the pastor's ultimatum. Not only would I have to tell the youth group that I was pregnant, but I'd also have to apologize for my indiscretions. I had explained to the pastor that I'd been raped, something I hadn't even told my parents.

It didn't seem to matter; my words fell on deaf ears. I justified it to myself by thinking about my ex-boyfriend, and how I'd only been held accountable for having sex with him to my parents. I'd never had to publicly apologize for that. With the shame still fresh from that, I rationalized that this was an overdue apology.

I accepted the fact that I'd have to tell everyone and apologize, even though I knew logically that I had nothing to apologize for in this case. I hadn't made a choice that could warrant my pregnancy; that choice had been taken away from me. But, I knew what had to be done. The day of, I was told that we would be meeting in the youth chapel. My peers and the church leadership would be present. I'd expected maybe forty or fifty people to potentially be there. I also knew that our senior pastor would make a special appearance at some point. If I apologized properly and showed my willingness to submit to authority, I'd be allowed to go on the trip with my friends.

I wanted to be allowed to escape from the emotion and heartache at home. I steeled myself on Wednesday as I walked inside. On my way in, I saw Kerri and Alia, who worriedly checked in with me. They knew what had to happen and wanted to ask if I was okay. We all knew it was an empty question; my answer that I was "all right" was just as empty. On the way in, my legs felt heavy and I started questioning my actions. What am I doing? I would go in there and essentially lie in an effort to be honest and comply with the pastor's instructions. What is happening? How would I go in there and apologize for something I didn't do? I kept thinking about how I did do it, just under completely different circumstances. Now I had to pay the price. It was a useless attempt at convincing myself, but I had to try.

Somehow, I managed to get inside. My parents were already there, sitting down. I had known they would be there, but I was still surprised to see them directly in the front row, saving an empty seat for me. It seemed like this had spiraled out of control—there was so much attention being paid, way more than I thought was warranted. I knew all of that attention would be on me. The anxiety nearly overwhelmed me, my heart pounding in my chest and my breaths coming fast. The urge to run suddenly shot through me: run, get out, escape, hurry!

But there was nowhere to go. This had to happen; this was going to happen. I needed to be brave. I struggled to get my bearings and control my breathing as I glanced around. I finally noticed how many other sets of parents were present. At the time, I didn't understand why they were needed, but in a way, I was glad to see them. If my parents had been the only ones, all of my peers would have shuffled in and known immediately that it was something to do with me.

The senior pastor had not yet arrived, and the youth pastor informed us that the senior pastor was currently making an announcement in the main church about this very meeting and we should expect him in about ten minutes, which is when we'd get started. At that point, there were between thirty to forty people in attendance, but within a few minutes, tons of people began swarming in. Parents, church leadership, people who were completely unrelated to the youth program, everyone seemed to be flooding the space. I blanched; what were all those people doing? Why was everyone coming in? I had no idea what was happening. I had only agreed to confide in my peers and their parents, not this enormous mass of churchgoers. Pretty soon, the small room was full, and it was standing room only. People sat where they could or stood, all with the same curiosity on their faces.

I found out later that the pastor had announced the meeting to the entire congregation. He'd invited everyone with children in junior high or high school, who had an interest in the church's youth, and stressed the importance of the meeting. It was no surprise that the majority of the congregation decided to attend. Sitting anxiously in the first row, I knew nothing of that, simply trying to calm my racing heart. Eventually, the pastor worked his way through the crowd up to the front. I knew the meeting was about me, but I didn't know what else he might be announcing or what he'd say. I didn't know whether he would use my story as a teachable moment, to show how God forgives sin, or how the church loves and supports each member of the community. I knew they would sit in judgement of me, but I hoped what he said would alleviate some of that and remind people that only God could judge.

"I'm glad you all were able to come here today. I've brought you here to discuss a very serious issue. One of our high school girls claims to serve God, yet she has found herself in complete sin, lies, and manipulation. She has acted as a role model and leader, but that has not been. Today, she is coming here to ask you all to forgive her. For you all to accept her apology for falsely representing herself as godly. Her parents are here as well. Though they love and support her, they do not support her sin. They are also here to listen as she apologizes to all of us for pretending to be something she was not and for being a poor example of a leader."

I blinked and looked over to my parents. I couldn't imagine how mind-boggling the situation was for them, how much hurt they had to be feeling, how protective of me they would be feeling. I know for a fact that they never expected anything to this extent; they wouldn't have agreed to shaming me in such a manner. Tears ran down my mother's face and my father's shoulders shook. His usually calm demeanor broke, and he seemed taken aback. They met my bewildered gaze, as if we were silently asking each other: How could this have happened? We never meant for it to be like this. They believed in being held accountable for our actions. They'd always taught me right from wrong, but they'd never used shame or guilt as a tool to enforce my behavior. They'd used forgiveness, compassion, and love, just as the Bible taught us. Before any of us could say anything aloud, the pastor continued.

"This individual is going to need to tell you that not only has she found herself in sin, but her sin has now resulted in her being three months' pregnant. At this time, Michelle, will you now come forward?"

The crowd's scattered gasps and murmurs were audible. Later, I realized people were more surprised at how the pastor outed me than any real shock at my actions. I stood up under the weight of everyone's eyes. I scanned the audience as I laboriously made my way up near the pastor. Some of the other girls were crying, some were laughing quietly. Some gave me looks that screamed "Oh, I figured."

Kerri and Alia cried for me. None of us had expected this. Even if it had actually been a sin, this was complete overkill. The fact that it had been rape made everything so much worse. We were horrified, but too young and inexperienced to know better. We'd never attended other churches; we couldn't have known that this wasn't standard practice.

It was no secret that many of my peers had been sexually active. We all knew, and we all talked about it. They sat there, undoubtedly worried themselves, wondering if they'd be next. It reminded me of The Scarlet Letter. I bore myself up as best I could and offered my apology, avoiding everyone's eyes and staring resolutely at the wall. I said I was sorry for not being a better leader and for falsely representing Christianity. Truthfully, I was sorry. It was real. I was sorry for the sex I'd had with the boyfriend I'd cared about. But I wasn't sorry about being raped, and I wasn't sorry that I'd become pregnant. No matter how hard I tried to hold on to the genuine guilt, it felt like an inauthentic sham.

I could hardly see through the tears streaming down my face, but most of them weren't for me. One glance could see how utterly broken my parents were, and I felt more shame in the hurt I caused them than anything else. My eyes darted around the gigantic congregation in front of me, witnessing my shame. I watched a mother subtly reach over and tap both of her sons, teenage boys, and signal them to leave with her. I heard another man reach for his daughter and ask her to go with him. I didn't understand why people were leaving. As it turned out, many people left the church that day, never to return. Plenty of parents worried that if their child found themselves in a similar situation, or any situation where they'd fallen short of the church's expectations, they'd also be ridiculed and made an example of.

For those who stayed, like myself, the pain went even deeper. I'd grown up in this church, listening to this pastor's sermons. I worshipped there, volunteered there with people I trusted and even loved. My mother worked there. This was yet another betrayal of that trust. That betrayal was far beyond anything I'd ever experienced. Beyond anything I knew how to handle or cope with. The trauma was unimaginable. In a few short months, I'd been shaken by the very foundations of a world I once found beautiful and safe. A world I'd thought only harmed bad people who deserved it. A world I could no longer understand.

With all that new emotion, I had a single thing driving me towards healing. A reason to live, to get healthy. I had to be healthy and strong for a singular purpose: the baby growing inside of me. A baby who didn't deserve any of this. He or she was perfect and they should be allowed to come into the world loved and welcomed. My mission was to protect this child. I lived for that mission, managing to survive that day and the ensuing days, no matter how difficult.

My next challenge came in the form of the adoption agency. My pastor had convinced my parents to reach out and get in contact with them and then to schedule the initial visit. They were planning to walk me through the legal specifics and the procedure itself. There were many parts of adoption to plan for: choosing the adoptive parents, filling out paperwork, arranging for counseling, figuring out medical insurance...it all made my head spin. I hadn't even decided that I wanted to go the adoption route! But I couldn't disobey my parents, and I wanted to be as fully informed as possible.

In the midst of all of the other confusing aspects, the agency aggressively asked me again and again for the identity of the biological father. I tried to explain that I didn't know who he was. It wasn't a lie; I'd seen his name tag at the restaurant, but that easily could have been a nickname or some kind of inside joke. There was no way to know anything else about him, and I obviously hadn't returned to the position since the assault. I'd never needed any more information about him, certainly not while I was working to forget him. Harder to forget a man whose name I knew.

I have no idea whether or not it was standard practice at the time, or if adoption agencies routinely do this nowadays, but the agency started making arrangements to run an advertisement in a local newspaper. They would be asking for a John Doe, fitting my vague physical description, who had had sexual contact with me. I tried to explain that I'd been raped, but either they didn't believe me or they just didn't care. I assumed it was lack of belief; after all, they were likely familiar with teenage girls pretending they'd been raped to salvage some dignity and not get in trouble with their parents. I balked at the idea. They would have to publish my information to find him, so it would be out in the world, and the number of crank callers or possible stalkers was mind-boggling. People might be able to find our house or where my parents worked and harass us...I resolutely would not allow that to happen.

I ended up calling my ex-boyfriend, Jason. I had slept with him pretty soon after the rape, so, in theory, he could be the father. I desperately wanted him to be the father. Deep in my heart, I probably knew it wasn't true, but I wanted to believe it. I explained to him that I was pregnant, and I was talking to an adoption agency. He was very kind and, when I explained the situation with the agency, he signed all of the papers as the biological father. I never said that he was the actual father and I, myself, went back and forth whether I could believe it or not, so we danced around the subject for a long time. Without any real confirmation one way or the other.

Not long after narrowly avoiding the humiliation of epic proportions that the adoption agency wanted to push on me, I went back to the restaurant where I'd used to work. I hadn't returned since the assault and it was difficult to walk up to those doors once more. However, I had to know. What was his name? Who was that manager? My stomach roiled in anxiety. I wasn't sure I wanted the answers. As it turned out, I wouldn't receive them. My friends had advised me to report the rape, but I would at least need his details to do so.

In a supreme twist of cosmic irony, he had apparently told all of my previous co-workers that I was a stalker. That I had been stalking him! They refused to give me any information at all. They wouldn't even tell me if the name on his nametag was a nickname or not. The incident would have shaken me if it hadn't been so ridiculous. An obviously sheltered, sixteen-year-old girl was supposedly stalking a full-grown man? When multiple people who'd been in the parking lot that night had seen him voluntarily get into my car and ask for a ride? Who likely had seen his predatory behavior towards other young girls working there? I shook my head in disgust and left, trying to put the whole incident out of my mind.

I was dealing with the emotional burdens even most adults aren't equipped to deal with, so I was ready to be sixteen again. The day of the DC trip finally arrived. I could not have been more excited. I was ready to go! I had taken time to process some of the trauma and felt ready to begin the process of moving on. I had no way of knowing what an enormous journey it would be, but the first step had to be something for me. After everything I'd been through, I deserved this ray of hope. I felt good. My friends would be there, and I knew we'd have a great time together. It felt like the change I needed to start living again.

I stood outside, holding my bag and getting ready to climb up into the van. Before I could, another youth pastor who would be coming on our trip with us tapped me on the shoulder and beckoned me aside. I followed, confused, but still enthusiastic and practically bouncing on the balls of my feet. I didn't know him super well, but he usually seemed friendly enough. He lowered his voice to a threatening tone.

"Hey, just so you know, if you tell anybody in the other youth groups that we're joining on this trip that you're pregnant and disgrace our group in that manner, you will be sent home immediately. Not only that, but your parents will be required to spend the money to fly you out from wherever we are across the country. You will not speak of this pregnancy. Do you understand?"

I knew what he was saying. Altogether, we'd be amongst over one hundred other kids, all of them strangers to me. I had no intention of saying anything to them, but having such an obvious threat dangled over my head raised my hackles. He knew my parents' financial situation; the entire church did. We didn't have the money for that. No way could they afford to suddenly pay hundreds of dollars to fly me home. The fact that he would threaten my family, who had done nothing wrong, as a representative of the church was unbelievable. They were our spiritual refuge and my mom's employer. The casual authority they wielded in that threat was hard to fathom. The entire trip was supposed to be a break for me, from my family and from the looming pregnancy. But then, he basically told me that I was not valued. I wasn't allowed to speak and had no control.

When something is taken from you—robbery, rape, or some other route—the loss of whatever was stolen feels raw. At that moment, he stole my voice. On top of everything else that had been stolen, by my manager and by my church, here he stood, taking one more thing from me. I had so little to hold on to. I couldn't muster any kind of rebuttal. I simply mouthed some placating words.

"Absolutely. I will not. I won't talk about it."

I loaded onto the bus, but the spring in my step was gone. Another casualty in the war of attrition life seemed determined to wage. We drove 22 hours that first day, and the second was eighteen hours. I was frequently queasy, a horrific combination of morning sickness and car sickness. I was terrified to explain why I needed to throw up, so I ended up ruining more than one sweatshirt while waiting for the next rest stop. People inevitably asked why I puked so much, and I couldn't tell them. I made up some story about being susceptible to motion sickness. Sometimes the bus would pull over for me, but I always felt like I was imposing. I started to wonder exactly why I'd been so keen to go on the trip at all.

By day three, we'd reached somewhere in Montana, and we were staying in a guest home. The owner belonged to a church we were partnered with who had graciously volunteered to host some of us for the night. There were four other girls besides myself staying there; the rest of our group were spread out in similar houses throughout the city. I suddenly started feeling some kind of unidentifiable pain in my stomach, something I wasn't familiar with. I wasn't positive, but they felt like menstrual cramps. I figured it was just something that happened while you're pregnant and maybe it meant I had to go to the bathroom. Just as I got inside, I realized the truth: they were contractions! I was bleeding everywhere.

As the blood flowed in rivulets down my legs, I stood there in shock. I realized too that I was in a stranger's house, surrounded by people I'd been forbidden from confiding in about the pregnancy. How was I supposed to get help without alerting them? My heart sank. It was a miscarriage. For some reason, the idea of a miscarriage had never occurred to me; I was a young, healthy girl. Something powerful shifted inside of me that moved me to tears. I cradled my belly and knelt down on the floor in my own blood and prayed, more fervently than I ever had before. I prayed that God would not take this baby from me.

This poor child, begot under such awful circumstances, now losing the battle of natural selection on the floor of a tiny bathroom. I squatted there, hoping against hope that it wouldn't end like this. There was no relief, no secret longing to erase all evidence of my rape. It wasn't that I couldn't suffer this last indignity; I simply couldn't bear that this life would be lost. This was the last straw for me. My reason to live, pooling on the floor around my knees.

"God, don't let me lose this baby. I don't want to lose this baby! I've already gone through so much pain. I've done the hard part. My family knows, the church knows. I've sacrificed my pride. What else would you have me do? I am begging you for this one thing! Please! Don't let my baby die!"

At that moment, the owner of the house hollered up the stairs. Everyone must have been awake. I was still there, lying on the freezing tile floor, bleeding and sweating profusely, clutching my stomach and mumbling

69

my prayers. The tile's coolness felt like relief. It was hard to know the right thing to do. I couldn't have known whether it would stop, if I needed to call an ambulance, how I could have explained to everyone what had happened, how my parents could possibly afford to fly me back to California...I didn't know anything. I lay there on the floor, my head spinning, as I tried to reason what to do. I focused on the house owner's words:

"Girls, girls, is there someone named Michelle? I need a Michelle. She has a phone call. Is there a Michelle here?"

I heard her, but I didn't understand. Why was she saying my name? Who could possibly be calling for me? Only the church leadership on the trip even knew where I was and it was so late. My body shook with another round of sharp pain and my vision swam.

"I-I'm in the bathroom!"

"Well, you have a phone call. I don't really appreciate people calling my house in the middle of the night!"

"I don't, I mean, I don't know anyone who would call me. I'm sorry."

She asked me if I would be able to grab the cordless phone. I felt weak and vulnerable, but knew I couldn't let her know what was happening. I affirmed I could and reached my arm through the door to grasp it. I was already thinking ahead to how I'd manage to clean up all of the mess I'd made. I thanked her absently and held up the phone to my ear.

"Hello?"

A man's voice greeted me across the line, someone I'd never heard before.

"Hey, are you Michelle?"

"Yeah, my name's Michelle…"

I trailed off, somewhat woozy and mainly confused.

"You don't know me. I'm from one of the other youth groups on this trip. I was woken from a dream and I saw a girl named Michelle who was very afraid that her baby would die. But God wants you to know that your baby will not die. Do you know anything about this?"

My head spun. I wondered if I was being tested and stayed silent.

"Does that make sense to you at all?"

"Yes, thank you."

I hung up, having no idea what else to do. I certainly didn't want to admit anything and I was worried I could pass out from the blood loss. Within moments of hanging up, the bleeding slowed and then stopped. I had no explanation for it other than a miracle. The cramps had also stopped and didn't return for the rest of the night. Or ever. I spent a long time meticulously scrubbing the floor and washing out my clothes. I was terrified I might ruin her towels because I knew that blood would stain.

That night, I bonded with my baby for the first time. I had to repay God for listening to me by ensuring this baby would have the best chance at life I could possibly provide. Before, the baby had been my purpose, as some kind of vague entity, but now I saw him or her as a person. Someone I wanted to love and cherish. We formed a bond that would never be broken. That bond is just as strong now, 31 years later.

I still don't know why I hemorrhaged that night, or why God chose a stranger to deliver such an important message of hope. More than recognizing the new bond with the baby, more than my desire to run home to the safety of my own mother's arms, that night I felt the comfort of my Heavenly Father. He healed my body and sent peace, love, and forgiveness to my heart. That night, I truly began my journey towards spiritual healing, a journey that I'll continue on for the rest of my life. Though I had never lost hope for myself, I renewed my commitment to my own health and well-being.

I had six months remaining, and I determined they would be the very best I could offer. Whether I ended up choosing parenting or adoption, and that choice would be mine to make, I wanted the world for this child. For my child. Everything I put in my body, anything that I did with it, would all be for the good of the baby growing inside of me. No opportunities would be denied. I had loved my child in an abstract, vague way, but now it felt tangible. Like there was a real person in me who would grow up with their own thoughts and feelings. That night, I stopped being a teenager who happened to be pregnant and truly became a mother.

I carried those thoughts with me, even as I enjoyed the following three weeks of the trip. I was able to swallow down the sickness and not let it weigh me down. We visited Mount Rushmore, the Statue of Liberty, the Twin Towers, the Smithsonian Institute, and the White House. I saw President George H.W. Bush as he walked his dog! I went to many amazing churches along the way and prayed for our country's prosperity. I had three wonderful weeks of solace from the heartache that had made up my past few months, and it was a welcome respite.

The trip eventually came to a close, and I knew I'd have to face reality again. I would return home, to my parents, my school, the daily humdrum. I'd have to deal with them saying adoption was the only way, and face the pastor pushing the same option. He had gone through the Christian adoption agency for his own daughter and undoubtedly directed my parents towards this same agency. I couldn't fault them; they were doing what they believed was right. They wanted what was best for me and the baby I carried. Going home meant facing all of that once more. Yet, I was excited to see my parents again, to tell them all that I'd seen and done. I had missed them and my brother; I loved them and was anxious to see them again. I could not stave off the dread in my heavy heart though, for I would be coming back to a new normal.

They picked me up when we arrived home and my mom excitedly asked how the trip was, before noticing that I was physically changed.

"Oh my goodness, your belly grew!"

It really had. I was now four months along and it was obvious with my current clothes. I now had a small pregnancy belly. Without thinking, I replied,

"I did, huh? It's kind of cute."

I didn't catch the look on her face, but she didn't reply. I realized that it probably wasn't cute to her. She cleared her throat and tried to tell me that I looked good. She wasn't unkind, but her heart definitely wasn't in it. I decided to be cheerful and change the subject.

"I have so much to tell you about my trip!"

"Yeah, we want to hear all about it. But, we have some news for you as well."

"What is it?"

"You're going to be moving to Los Angeles. About three hours from where we live. You'll be staying with our pastor's sister and her family for the rest of your pregnancy."

I knew they meant the senior pastor, who had forced me to apologize and humiliated me in front of the entire congregation.

"...but I don't know them."

My mother hastened to reassure me. "They're really nice! They'll have a great place for you. They have a three-year-old son."

"What about school? My friends?"

"You'll go to school there, of course. You'll make new friends, you're young and charming. After the baby is born, you'll come home."

"Why? Why am I leaving? What did I do wrong? Why are you punishing me like this? What's the reason?"

They couldn't give me a satisfactory answer then. Likely, they were pressured by our pastor and feared the ridicule I would inevitably endure at the hands of my peers. Maybe, they thought no one would know about the pregnancy this way and my reputation would be spared. Not to mention, the adoption agency they were so keen on me using was based out of LA. The agency had promised counseling for me and perhaps they thought it could be facilitated more easily if I lived there too. I've always known that my parents love me and I trusted them in this, as in everything else. They were doing the right thing, by their standards. I never agreed that this was the correct choice, but I knew they were hurt and confused and had sought guidance.

They gave me two weeks from the time I got home to pack my belongings and say my farewells. I would have to go away and become a mother alone, without even Kerri or Alia to rely on. Far away from the people who knew and loved me. Meanwhile, my friends would start our junior year without me. When I returned, I would be a mom.

# FOUR

# *Undefined by Authority*

*"Then I returned and considered all the oppression that is done under the sun: And look! The tears of the oppressed, But they have no comforter— On the side of their oppressors there is power, But they have no comforter."*
*(Ecclesiastes 4:1)*

It was hard to wrap my head around the impending move. In an effort to introduce me to my new surroundings and to help me with settling in, my mom and I went to Los Angeles to register me at my new school and meet the family I'd be living with. As we drove through the neighborhood and rolled up to the school, it was immediately apparent just how different it would be compared to my old school. It was a very upper-class neighborhood. The expensive cars glistened in the sunlight, newly polished. Our 1969 Chevy Malibu was glaringly out of place.

When we arrived at the school, we were directed to the principal's office. We sat down on oversized brown chairs facing the principal himself, a broad-shouldered, dark-haired man with a thick Magnum P.I. mustache.

He quietly tapped a pencil on his sturdy oak desk, purposefully projecting an intimidating aura. He waited awhile to speak, then commented that it was a unique situation. Ideally, he wanted to offer an alternative to attending regular classes. My mother's eyes narrowed and she cut him off, declaring her intent to enroll me at the school for a normal schedule. He cleared his throat and argued that it would be difficult for me, and he worried about my ability to succeed in school. I crossed my arms, somewhat offended by the implications, but not altogether sure that he was wrong.

My mom rebutted him, launching into a heartwarming speech about how she admired the fact that I was not afraid to face the ridicule and judgement I knew would surely come. I was actually a little afraid, but that hardly mattered in the face of her pride. She was proud of me. She didn't have to say it aloud; I knew she was. Even as I sat there, unconsciously cradling the small protrusion of my stomach, I knew she was proud. The principal tried hard to talk her out of her decision, my decision. Yet, I sat there silently, with no opportunity to advocate for myself.

My mom hadn't bothered to ask me what my preference was, and the principal never so much as glanced in my direction during the entire conversation. I believed it was an adult matter, and I was still just a kid. I watched as they went back and forth, frustration bubbling beneath the increasingly strained polite smiles traded. Ultimately, we won when my mom reminded him that it is illegal to withhold education from a willing student. With reluctance from both parties, they eventually agreed to consider a modified on-campus schedule.

With that out of the way, we went home again and I returned to figuring out how I would make this move. I had told my friends about it; Kerri and Alia were obviously as disappointed as I was. After all these years, Alia still resents the fact that I had to leave during such a vulnerable time for me. They kept asking me why I had to leave, but I didn't know. I gave weak answers, citing the adoption agency's location in LA and how the pastor's sister and her family were planning to help me get spiritual and emotional counseling through that agency. I knew it was what my parents thought was best. The answers weren't satisfying for me to give or my friends to hear. Many years later, my mom clarified that they really had sent me away to protect me; they'd been worried about the judgement and ridicule I'd likely receive at my school, both during and after my pregnancy.

At one point, Alia asked if I was really going to give the baby up for adoption. I told her no, just that I hadn't yet informed my parents of my decision. We all knew the truth: I wasn't brave enough to confront them about it.

As I continued my preparations to leave, I began to feel a new emotion very keenly. It wasn't easily recognizable, and it wasn't familiar to me. I didn't have the words for it at the time, but I know now what I felt: abandonment. No matter how much I trusted my parents and believed in their love for me, I was being sent away, shunned from the family. Part of my preparations included trying to come to terms with that abandonment and trying to overcome the anxiety of starting at a new school when I clearly would not fit in. I would be the only pregnant teenager on a large campus full of privilege. It didn't help that I came from such modest means. Even under the best of circumstances, I wouldn't have been able to relate to the other students. I didn't have designer clothes, and my bright yellow 1979 Plymouth Arrow would stand out in a sea of expensive, sporty cars. My father had generously passed it down to me so I would have transportation, but it was now forever tainted by memories I was still desperate to forget.

I invited my dad to come down to LA with me to get a new paint job for the car. I'd been saving up the sixty bucks needed, and he was happy to be asked along on such a venture. We ended up having a really fun day together. We drove the three hours down, talking about everything and nothing; simply enjoying each other's company. I knew after the move that it would be months before I had a chance to just be around him again.

After we arrived at the body shop, we dropped off the car and had a few hours to kill while it was painted. We went for a walk around to see the area. As we headed up a long road, I idly wondered if he was ashamed to walk next to me now that I had begun to show. I didn't have to wait long for a definitive answer. After nearly a mile, some jerk called out a crude comment. I didn't hear what was said, but my father did. He stopped dead in his tracks and turned to me.

"You don't ever need to let others decide who you are. You get to choose who you will be."

He'd always been a man of few words, so I listened carefully. The words had a powerful impact on me, then and to this day. That was a pivotal moment in my life and one I remember constantly. No matter what people have taken from me, what they say or do, or how they try to define me, I know that nobody gets to decide who I am except me. I remain undefined by others, even now. The only judgement that matters is God's and my own. I could see on his face how much my dad loved me, how none of what had happened to me or what I'd done marred his pride. He wasn't embarrassed to be seen with me or to be my father. Furthermore, I knew the worst I could do would be to bow my head under the weight of my guilt. If I remained true to myself, my beliefs, and character, I had something that can't be taken. I had hope. I had joy. I had a bright future, full of health and prosperity. Then and now, I am so much more than the sum of my losses.

I held on to that moment when the day of the move finally arrived. My bags were packed, my newly painted car loaded, and I was as ready as

I'd ever be. This time, saying goodbye meant driving alone down to Los Angeles. It meant a new school and spending my first night in my new room. My first night in a house full of strangers. I tried to enliven my mindset, telling myself it was me and baby, out to conquer the world! It was an adventure, just for us. I squared my shoulders and began my journey.

Having only gained my driver's license a few months prior, and learned in a much smaller town, the five-lane highways were daunting. I'd never driven in a big city by myself. I started missing the two lanes from back home and spiraled into missing everything from home. I was only a couple hours into the journey and I already wanted to turn around. Every mile I drove was another step into an adult's adventure, into motherhood, and I was rudely reminded that I was very much still a child. As the gauge ticked upwards, I unknowingly merged into the carpool lane. Where I'd grown up, carpool lanes hadn't existed, so I wasn't on the look-out for them or cognizant of their meaning.

Suddenly, blue and red flashing lights appeared in my rearview mirror. I'd never been pulled over before, and nerves spiked. Exactly what I needed on my first night alone: some interaction with the police. It was difficult to maneuver through the five lanes over to the shoulder, but I pulled over as soon as I could. I was shaking and my breathing was unsteady. I couldn't figure out what I'd done wrong; my eyes had been firmly locked on my speedometer. I wasn't speeding. He got out and walked up to my window, intimidating.

"Do you know why I pulled you over?"

I blurted out, "I wasn't speeding!"

"No, you weren't. License and registration."

I pulled it out with trembling hands.

"You were in the carpool lane."

The title meant nothing to me. I could have reasoned it out normally, but I was so anxious I could barely think enough to respond.

"Okay? But I wasn't speeding."

"No. It means you have to have at least two people in your car, ma'am."

I looked up at him, with as much courage and conviction as I could muster and replied:

"I do have two people in the car. My baby and me."

That wasn't an excuse in the eyes of Californian law. It's easy to look back and dismiss that as a very loaded political response, but I didn't mean it that way. I had placed my hand over my ever-expanding baby bump and felt triumphant; it was the first time I had taken ownership of my baby and advocated for us together. At a time when my voice had been denied over and over again, it was a relief to be able to speak up, even when it was scary. I took pride in how I defended us and gave my child value. The officer simply shook his head and ended up letting me off with a warning, unwilling to engage in a legal debate over whether life starts at conception or birth.

"Will you just stay out of the carpool lane until your baby is born? Please?"

I quickly agreed and happily went on my way, thinking about how big of a moment it had been for me. It was the first in a long line of decisions I got to make for the safety of myself and my baby.

I used the notes and maps my dad had written me to finally find my destination. Upon parking, I spoke aloud to my baby, rubbing my stomach as I did so. I promised my sweet angel that we would make the most of our new house. I prayed to God for the strength to walk through those unfamiliar doors and to embrace this new family. I asked that my family be kept safe during my absence. I wanted to make this work.

Shelly and Tony, the pastor's sister and her husband, were very kind to me. They welcomed me into their home and showed me the room they had prepared for my arrival. Despite such niceties, I felt lost in a strange world, so far from my own. Their son, Jeffrey, was adorable and a happy presence, but he wasn't my brother and they weren't my parents. They allowed me to settle in and put away my clothes before letting me know that I would be allowed to make two phone calls home a week and I had to keep each call under five minutes.

In 1989, it would be the only contact I had with my friends and family besides mail. If I exceeded the time limit, they would ask my parents to send extra money to cover the expenses. I knew my parents didn't have more money, especially not to spend on needlessly excessive phone calls. I didn't want to burden them any more than I already had. I was indebted to Shelly especially; she was a nurse, and the doctor she worked for agreed to monitor my pregnancy and make sure everything went smoothly.

That move marked the end of summer and, all too soon, I had to register for my classes. I made my way back to the school of wealthy kids for a scheduled appointment to make everything official. No sooner had I shouldered open the large entry doors than my attention was called to the school nurse. She was an older, soft-spoken woman.

"Hello, sweetie! You must be Michelle. I knew you were going to come in. Come with me!"

She led me down the halls until we arrived at a door with a large sign declaring it to be the nurse's office. I was confused—shouldn't I have been at the registration office? She insisted that she just wanted to talk with me first. I wasn't sure, but, at that point, most of my supposed decisions had been made by the adults around me, and I wasn't inclined to argue with her. She explained to me that there had been a meeting with the district and school leadership about having a pregnant student enroll.

"Since the day I found out that you would be coming, I have had you in my heart and in my prayers. I wanted to find you right away to tell you that I am here for you. If you need anything, tell me. I'm going to be here for you if you're not feeling well, if people aren't being kind, or if you just need to get away from everything for a while. If you need a safe space, I'm here. This is your place."

I was taken aback by her kindness. I couldn't express how thankful I was for her and for God sending this lovely woman into my life. I did not yet know how important she would be to me in the months to come. How her generosity would be a catalyst for the years of healing I would go through. At the time, overcome by emotion, my words were few. I think I smiled and thanked her.

"You're going to hear a lot of other things today, and I'll let you get on with all of that, but I wanted to swoop you up before they got to you, and I just wanted to let you know that you aren't alone."

All of this, without knowing me or my story. Tears of happiness pricked at my eyes. I genuinely believed that she would help me and could only guess at how many times I'd find myself in her office. She gently showed me out and directed me to the registrar. There, I found a very different environment. Like with the nurse, they all knew me by name and reputation, but unlike her, they saw me as a problem. I bounced from one office to another, speaking with counselors, registration clerks, the vice principal, and, finally, the principal himself. There was no privacy; other students milled around, trying to pretend like they weren't eavesdropping, desperate for the gossip on the pregnant girl.

Sitting across from the principal, he looked just as I remembered him, pencil in hand. We shook hands stiffly.

"Nice to see you again," he lied. "Well, I've brought you here to, uh, welcome you to the school."

"Thank you."

"And to let you know that we have a really good at-home education program, and I really believe this is right for you. You can stay home! You clearly need to take care of your body and this gives you the chance to relax, rest, and continue the pregnancy."

My mom wasn't there to advocate for me. She didn't know that he would go behind her back when she wasn't there, go back on the agreement they'd reached only a week before. It was just me, intimidated by this authority figure who was, once again, trying to take my decisions out of my hands. But, I knew what I needed.

"I don't want to be home. That's the last thing I want to do."

It's not even my home I thought, though I didn't say.

"...in addition to our concern for you, we're also, of course, concerned about the reputation of this school and this could cause an epidemic."

An epidemic? Are you kidding me? As if I was the host of some deadly disease, that I should be quarantined like a leper! That my pregnancy might somehow "infect" his precious privileged students. My response was laden with sarcasm.

"I want to come to school. I can certainly guarantee you that I will not be getting anyone pregnant!"

Once more, I advocated for what I felt was best. For me and my baby. It still wasn't huge, but that's what I had. I knew that every decision I made for me would impact my baby too. He sighed, almost comically loud.

"Well, if you insist on attending school, we'll look at a modified schedule. You don't need to be here all day. We can probably do three classes."

I could see that I had to be very firm with him.

"I want to graduate on time. I'm a junior in high school now. I don't want to fall behind. I'm willing to be here, put in the work, and grow. Maybe I'll be embarrassed about what I look like. I'm willing. You need to educate me. That's the law."

He reluctantly agreed and shuffled me off to tour the classrooms. I noticed that no one else was getting a tour, but I didn't object. An assistant showed me the desks in the classrooms and explained that the school was worried I wouldn't fit in the desks as I continued to get larger.

"It's going to be really hard for you to be here. We can't make modifications to the desks, so I really want you to reconsider attending in person. We can do homeschool, don't forget that."

The entire campus was at least three times the size of my old school, and she had me walk everywhere. She kept asking if it was too hard, if I was winded, and reminding me that I would only continue to grow larger and further along. It was increasingly frustrating as I realized what she was doing, what they were all doing. I did my best to keep my temper in my pocket, but I'm not proud to say that I snapped at one point, saying:

"I'm only sixteen. I think my body can do just fine with walking and sitting at desks. There are fat people in this school who are bigger than I'll ever get!"

Needless to say, she had no response to that. Eloquently or not, I had made my case. My classes were in order. But, convincing the principal again to let me attend the school and register wasn't my only challenge in those final days leading up to the start of junior year. As most teenage girls will tell you, a crucial part of school is clothes. The trends may have been different, but the need to look cute remained the same. It was especially difficult knowing that most students would be showing up in their designer duds and I'd be showing off my mom's extra-large shirts and elastic waistbands straining around my hefty stomach. Every time I looked through my scanty wardrobe, I was starkly reminded of the fact that even the largest clothes I'd packed were quickly getting too small on me. My mom knew I'd need maternity clothes, and sent me a card in the mail with $100 to spend.

I couldn't believe it! I knew how costly it was to send me that money and, for a second, I felt as if I was back home, in her arms. She'd always been the one to buy my clothes every year, and she likely felt my absence as keenly as I did. I took that precious card in hand and headed down to the local mall to begin my search. It was enormous! So much bigger than the mall I was used to. I was confident I'd be successful. Someone had to carry cute clothes I could afford. Armed with that newfound wealth and my confidence,

I strode into the first store. Automatically, I found myself in the junior's section. I laughed to myself quietly at the familiarity of it. I saw another girl, around my age, arguing with her mom about a belly shirt she wanted. Her mom thought that it wouldn't meet her school's dress code while she insisted that it would. I had a passing thought that I wasn't so different from that girl. I was also shopping for a belly shirt…

Wishing my worries were on the same scale, I looked for store signs pointing to a maternity section. I frowned, seeing none. I meandered around the shop for a while, but wasn't able to find anything. I figured I could start in the plus size section for now. They had a minimal selection, and everything screamed blatantly uncool. I saw shirts and dresses in pastel, with lace and floral designs. It looked like I'd be aging myself at least fifty years in them! I had no idea how limited my options truly were. I hoped that a larger department store would have a better selection, but my hopes were soon dashed. Cute maternity clothes didn't come into vogue until the early 2000s, and I was eleven years too early.

I managed to find one pair of stretchy blue maternity pants and several plus size t-shirts, one in every color: bright pink, turquoise, yellow, light pink, light blue, and black. Unfortunately, the arm holes on all of them were too big for my thin arms. I'd have to wear a tank top under them so my bra wouldn't show when I raised my arms and violate the dress code. The absolute last thing I needed was to get in any trouble at school. None of that had anything on buying maternity underwear. They were gigantic! I held them up, wondering if my butt would ever be that large. The size seemed right, but there was no way they were for a teenage girl. Of course, they weren't. They were for fully grown women. I wondered if I'd ever be able to shop in the junior section again after this. Would my body be permanently changed? At sixteen, even before the pregnancy, I hadn't fully matured into a woman yet. I took a deep breath and stopped that line of thought; it was depressing and scary. I refocused on the day's work. After all, I still needed to find matching socks and hair scrunchies!

All of my hard work led up to that fateful first day of school. I pulled into the parking lot with my bright white compact car, feeling snazzy in my new blue shirt, blue pants, and matching accessories. My confidence lessened slightly when I had to park between a purring black BMW and a cherry red Corvette. I saw teenagers driving sports cars, luxury cars, and knew, once again, that it was hardly just my belly that would stand out. The looks and whispers started long before I stepped out of the car. Although the hit teen drama Beverly Hill 90210 would not come out until the next year, what I experienced could have come straight out of the screen.

I gave myself a little pep talk. I was going to do this. And I would do it right. On my terms. No way would I let the principal bully me into homeschooling! I wanted to be here. I was excited. It would work; I could make this work. I hadn't yet managed to convince myself when I walked through the doors. I was almost six months' pregnant at that point, and all the clothes in the world couldn't have hid my condition. I endured whispering, giggling, shocked faces, pointed fingers, everything I could have imagined and some things that I hadn't. The principal had been so eager to tell us that there had never been a pregnant student before and the reactions seemed to confirm that. Whether that was entirely true was up for debate, but the school had obviously never seen anyone so far along.

Nausea rose in my throat, and I started questioning the wisdom of my decision. Why did I want this again? I could be homeschooled. It wouldn't be fun in a stranger's house, but at least there were only a few of them and they were sympathetic. I could easily spare myself the ridicule and judgement. Just as I contemplated the easier route, I saw a smiling face. Nurse Patty! I smiled back, appreciating the value she gave me. She waved me into her office and asked if I needed anything, probably recognizing the unsure look I sported. She reassured me that she was there for me. She even complimented my outfit and offered me some saltines to calm my stomach. I already trusted this godsend of a woman. This would be the first of many such visits. Sometimes it was just to lay down, or to talk to someone I knew had accurate information, or to weigh myself. Her office was a safe haven.

Later, as I walked through the halls to my second period class, face after face was unfamiliar and new. Dozens of people's conversations would hush when I turned towards them, people I hadn't grown up with and didn't know from Adam. Who had more money than I could fathom. Yet, somehow, I identified with them, with their teenage whims. After all, I was just like them. Or was I? Caught up in my own musings, I was taken unawares by a voice calling out my name. At first, I couldn't imagine that anyone would recognize me, and I do have a common name. But then, to my amazement, in the sea of faces, I saw a familiar one! JJ, an old friend from church back home. She and her family had moved away when her father had gotten a new job, a year or two before. Suddenly, I was no longer alone.

JJ introduced me to her group of friends. They seemed to be willing to accept me, maybe just for her sake, but I appreciated their welcome nonetheless. They had tons of questions about my pregnancy, wincing or getting grossed out at some of my answers, but also interested in the joy I found. Some of them likely looked forward to becoming a mother in their own time, but others were simply curious. JJ took me to football games, and I began attending her church. It was a really great way to build the connections in LA that would help me so much. It was familiar and fun. There were youth functions and outings where I was accepted wholeheartedly and was able to enjoy. I felt loved, without the condemnation or judgement I'd come to expect from a church.

Throughout my pregnancy, and in the years beyond, I felt that God had sent me many people who reminded me of my strength and helped through my weakness. They eased my healing and facilitated my renewed commitment to life. Some lasted months, others a lifetime. In the weeks that followed, I did struggle to fit in the chairs and to walk around the campus. Multiple bathroom breaks a day would delay me to my classes, but I found the strength to endure. I now had allies to catch me when I stumbled.

# FIVE

# *Undefined by Broken Promises*

*"Beloved, do not believe every spirit, but test the spirits, whether they are
of God; because many false prophets have gone out into the world."
(1 John 4:1)*

I had heard that pregnant women could experience strange food cravings, but nothing prepared me for the bizarre things I wanted to eat. One day, I desperately wanted an icy treat, but nothing seemed to satisfy. I wanted the tanginess of citrus and the salty taste of canned fish. In the end, I used an ice cube tray to make a strange concoction. I placed canned, chunky sardines in the pockets and then poured orange juice over them and shoved toothpicks in, freezing them to make OJ sardine popsicles. I'd never seen anything like it before or since. The idea popped into my head almost randomly and I made them, though I know the thought would make most people sick to contemplate. But, I enjoyed them, and they satisfied.

I confessed my strange concoction to Nurse Patty the next time I went to visit, and she giggled, enjoying my description. I'd gone in to lay down because my feet were swollen and my legs hurt. I'd repeatedly assured the principal and his assistants that I'd be able to walk the campus without a problem, even later in my pregnancy, but truthfully, some days, I couldn't make it all day. Nurse Patty welcomed me into her office and let me stay there all the way through lunch. She even went out to buy lunch for both of us, giving me a rare treat. We ate companionably and she gave me a lot of honest advice. She told me about the adoption process, much more in depth than the agency had, and how the birth mom was allowed to choose the terms of the adoption plan. On the other hand, she was surprisingly informative and supportive about my other option: parenting. Nurse Patty made sure I knew about social services and what they offered for very young, unemployed mothers. I took note of all of her words of wisdom; it was the first time an experienced adult had sat down and had a frank conversation with me about my options. I appreciated it, more than she knew.

When I was seven months along, it came time for an ultrasound. I bought a brand new VHS tape and brought it to the appointment when they said I could record it. I arrived early, unable to contain my excitement any longer. If all went well, for the first time, I would know whether the angel I'd been carrying for so long was a boy or girl. I tried to wait patiently for them to call me in, but my leg was bouncing with nerves. Before then, I'd been content with either option. Having a boy would offer a special connection, similar to the one I'd enjoyed with my younger brother. Together we could ride bikes, go skating or hiking, and play sports. If I had a girl, we could relate on a very different level. I could give her an understanding of her future, of being a woman in the world we live in. I imagined movies, shopping excursions, long walks, and car rides chatting. All of the experiences I'd had with my own mother.

Soon, they called my name. I jumped up and hurried inside, unable to stand another second of not knowing. I had to endure yet another pelvic exam first, to check my health and that of the baby. They never got any easier; they were so invasive and a little painful. I tried to focus on finally knowing my baby's sex to distract me from the exam. Ultrasounds in 1989 were difficult to parse for everyone not trained in the medical field. It mostly looked like a black and grey blur. Of course, I pretended that I knew what I was looking at, not wanting to seem more immature than my age gave away. The nurse moved the cold, gooey instrument over my belly. I ooh-ed and ah-ed at all of the right moments, nodding at body parts I definitely could not see. What was important was that I could see my baby and we were both healthy.

The nurse identified the baby's head and measured it, as well as its stomach, and length. She checked the heartbeat and said it was strong. I hadn't been concerned about the heartbeat before, but I was nonetheless reassured to hear that. We confirmed that my due date was still my seventeenth birthday, something that had long caused me flutters of anxiety and exhilaration. At one point, she showed me the nose, mouth, and it all still looked like a blur, but I loved every moment. Every part of that baby blur was mine! Finally, I couldn't contain myself any longer and I asked the pivotal question: boy or girl?

"Well, with the heartbeat and everything I've seen I think I know already, but I'll check now."

She dripped more of the cool liquid on my overheated skin, even though there was so much that it pooled in my lower back. I felt like I was sloshing around on the bed. She placed the scanner back on my stomach and made some adjustments, moving right and left, before speaking again.

"Ah, yes. I was correct! It's a girl!"

The announcement was simple; the message was huge.

Though I'd had no preference before, when she told me I carried a girl, I just melted like the ultrasound goo. Tears rolled down my face as I felt such overwhelming joy. I knew that, no matter what my ultimate decision would be, my baby would understand. She'd know everything I went through to give her the best life possible. I clutched the tape in my euphoric hands and, over the next few weeks, watched it over and over again, reliving that moment of pure, unfettered joy. I still never knew what I was looking at, but it didn't matter. I bonded with the baby inside of me, my daughter. I fell even more deeply in love with her, now that I knew enough to start thinking about her name. It felt more real than ever before. I wondered what her hair would look like, what color her eyes would be...the possibilities were endless.

Several months prior, I'd begun keeping a journal. I would document my day: my feelings, questions, and fears. I shared her kicks to my ribs and her pushing on my bladder so hard I thought it would burst. I speculated on paper about our future. I doodled and played with name options for her, writing them multiple times in different colors. Sarah and Ashley were my top two picks. From early on, my journal exposed my secret: that I planned to keep my baby. I wanted to raise her myself. As the months passed, my love for her grew stronger on every page. The further I fell in love with her, though, the more I questioned my ability to properly mother her. Could I be the mother she deserved? At the end of each passage, I remained confident in myself and my parental capabilities, even as a teenager. I knew it wouldn't be easy, but I was still so sure that I could make it work.

I kept telling myself and my baby we're going to figure this out, we're going to conquer the world! Together, we can do this! I don't care what the world says, we'll find a way! The invincibility of being a teenager flowed through my veins and mingled with my desire to get to know my daughter. I tried to prepare myself for the eventuality of being a mom, but all the information and maturity in the world couldn't really have made me ready. Thoughts of money, insurance, buying groceries, diapers, toys, car seats, and everything else we would need swirled around my head, no matter how many mantras I recited. They were never far from my mind. But I was going to find a way! I refused to get bogged down in the "how"s and focused on my daughter. However, thoughts of money and necessities weren't the only things weighing on me.

Having only had a brief meeting with the adoption agency, months ago in my hometown, I wondered why exactly I had been forced to move all the way to Los Angeles. I was promised counseling, peer-to-peer networking, and a personal social worker to walk me through the process, none of which I received. Now, in my last trimester, I was alone to consider the possibilities for my daughter and decide what would be best. How could I be trusted to do so when I hardly even knew what was best for me? I was still a child.

I knew my parents wanted me to choose adoption, and they had specific reasons for that. They hoped I would go on to graduate high school, attend college, get married, have a career, and then have children. The pregnancy completely flipped their order of things and took them by surprise. Adoption was a way to escape the interruption and resume the plan. Adoption was a solution to bring their daughter back home, still just a teen, only responsible for herself, and able to live the life they wanted for her. I understood all that and never resented them for it. After all, I had to consider the same question: what was the life I wanted my daughter to live?

While still their little girl, I now had the same responsibilities as them. The same dilemma. How best to protect and love my daughter? To give her what she needs and to remember that I had needs as well. I had been going along with the adoption plan for months by this point. "Yes" and "sure" were no longer enough. If I didn't start making real decisions and have the courage to stand up for those choices, then this decision would be made for me. It practically had been already and if I didn't do something soon, my "yes" and "sure" would whisk my daughter right out of my arms. I needed to begin thinking for myself and planning our future. With only months left to consider, I knew my time to finalize this life-changing decision was rapidly dwindling. But, maybe it could wait one night more.

That particular night, JJ wanted to take me to a football game at our school. I had paused in my attempts to get ready, hyper-analyzing everything I'd done up to that moment. I went back to getting dressed, to wondering what color shirt would look cutest. The first decision I made was to give myself permission to have one last night before sitting down and meditating long and hard on the right thing to do. I wouldn't know whether any of them were the right decisions. But, that night, I forcibly focused on thoughts that I could manage, on just enjoying a night out with friends as a normal, high school girl. The kind of night that I fervently hoped my daughter would be able to enjoy some day, surrounded by loving friends and family, supported on every side.

With my protruding belly leading the way, I lumbered from the parking lot to the football field. Every step was hard and I was annoyed that I'd had to park so far away. JJ was probably already seated with a few friends. I'd have to find them in a sea of people, all young and beautiful, decked out in our school colors. We had agreed to meet near the left side bleachers, but now the entire operation seemed impossible. As I approached the crowd, I realized that I would have to muscle my way through to reach my destination. Ducking and maneuvering my body, squeezing next to people, was no easy task. My feet ached, and I began to regret coming.

My body no longer felt lithe and irrepressible, the way a sixteen-year-old ought to feel. I was heavy, awkward, and definitely not cute. The opposite of how I wanted to feel at a high school event. As I waddled past a group of unfamiliar faces, packed so tightly that my belly was nearly hidden in the chaos, a boy my age caught my eye and called out:

"Hey there, gorgeous!"

As quickly as the words came out, I took a few steps out of the press of bodies and he could see my stomach. He must have caught a glimpse, because I saw his face pale abruptly and he scrambled, eyes darting around to think of a way out of the awkward moment. The comment had obviously been intended for me, but I pretended I hadn't heard. I politely excused myself as I continued past him. I overheard the guys who were with him, hassling and teasing him for the offhand compliment. They weren't trying to be quiet; they hadn't even waited for me to get out of earshot before raking me over the coals with crude phrases. I held onto my father's words about not letting others define me and refused to let those words penetrate my heart.

I barely held back tears and asked God to help me. I wanted to run, to get away from everyone and their judgmental eyes, cruel rumors, and implications. Even without the crowd, my body wouldn't let me run. I took a few deep breaths, trying as hard as possible to blink back the urge to cry. Just as I did so, my prayers were answered when I heard JJ.

"Michelle! We're over here!"

I made my way towards her, relieved. Despite that, I couldn't help the nagging wonder at the back of my mind. Would I ever be a normal teenager again? Or, even more importantly, would anyone ever want to marry me? I had dreamed my whole life of being both a mom and a wife. Had all of this taken away that hope? I forcibly stopped that train of thought. Even if I'd lost that, I could live with it. My daughter was worth it. I enjoyed that night, gossiping with the girls and cheering the teams on. The distraction was well worth the trouble, but, once I'd gotten home again, the same thoughts came back, stronger than before.

I agonized over what I could provide as a mother. The costs and benefits of adoption. I was significantly hindered by my lack of personal experience, my lack of worldly knowledge. It had to be my decision, made with as sober a mind as I could manage, but, in hindsight, it's tragically humorous that a child could be expected to predict so much with so little information available. Where were the people who could tell me things in an unbiased manner? All of the adults I'd spoken to had been frank in their support of adoption. Alia and Kerri, my friends, and my peers advocated for keeping the baby. Maybe that should have told me something, but no teenager ever wants to admit they don't know best. That they have barely grown up mentally, even if they have physically.

Deep in the mire of my indecision, the adoption agency finally contacted me. They probably realized that they needed to get in touch with me since the pregnancy would soon come to a close, and they had no real commitment from me. I scheduled an appointment for the following week, but I was very unsettled. It never sat well with me that they didn't believe my story. They must not have, if they were so willing to push for me to publicly expose myself in the local paper to find the monster who raped me. I couldn't imagine that they actually believed that I was raped; more likely they thought I'd had anonymous consensual sex. Even how they still assured me that the baby was most likely not his, due to my supposed promiscuity. Well, they weren't totally wrong on that front. My decisions at some points had been skewed and not driven by logic. Sometimes, I wasn't sure what the truth was anymore. The reality was that I had a baby who demanded mature, grown-up choices to be made, and I couldn't let her down.

I was willing to listen to the adoption agency. I was willing to take a responsible step forward, to consider all of my options, for both of us, but mostly for her. When the day arrived, my anxiety was running high, and I knew I had to be strong. My guard was up, and I had to be ready for whatever would come. Sacrificing my own desires didn't come naturally at sixteen, but I knew it was necessary. The love growing in my heart superseded anything I'd ever felt before. That love had helped me understand my parents' pain.

Geared up for whatever they'd throw my way, I made my way to the lunch meeting. I met the same social worker as before: Brenda. When she pulled up in her brown Nissan, my stomach churned in anticipation. I smiled anyway. She was very casual, discussing the traffic, that she'd have to remember to fill up the tank, and how she was absolutely famished. The small talk was something of a relief. We ordered food and sat down. I continued to listen as she chattered on. I wondered when the dialogue would turn towards more serious matters. It turned out to be a relatively long wait; we'd already finished eating and the food had been cleared. I hadn't wanted to bring it up, but by that point I wasn't really listening to her chit-chat. Unexpectedly, she reached into her purse for an envelope, which she then passed to me.

"What's this?"

"Oh that's money for you to buy maternity clothes."

I gave her a strange look. I'd spent the entirety of our lunch sitting across from her wearing what could only have been maternity clothes. I was already eight months pregnant at this point; did she think I hadn't needed new clothes before then? I patiently explained that I'd already bought some, gesturing at my outfit for the day. She brushed off the comment and told me to buy more. That it was part of the process. By process, I assumed she meant the adoption, and that someone presumably paid for this. I wasn't sure who that someone could be; I hadn't chosen adoptive parents. I hadn't even been shown prospective parents. I hadn't even confirmed that I wanted to choose adoption! I hesitated and declined the money, finally telling her that I wasn't sure I'd choose adoption after all. She dismissed my demur entirely and told me not to worry, that the money was for me to use as I wished.

"The adoption agency will be paying for all of your medical bills as well, so you needn't worry about that either. Is there anything else?"

Frazzled and frustrated, I stared at her blankly. She wasn't offering guidance, answers, networking, comfort, or even hope. She wasn't even listening to me, when she let me get a word in edgewise. All she could give me was financial help for very short-term costs. Even at the tender age of sixteen, I knew that wasn't enough. I didn't have the words to express my dissatisfaction completely, but she seemed to sense something was wrong.

"You have plenty of time to make your decision, but, in the meantime, let's get you some new clothes! Let us take care of you. We know you're not able to take care of yourself."

Her words were just as casual as bemoaning the traffic. She hardly seemed to give them much thought. The fact that it was so obvious to her that I couldn't care for myself...she was an expert in this situation. How could I hope to care for a child when no one would treat me like I was anything but a child? I hated it, but she wasn't incorrect.

The rest of the meeting was uneventful; she made some empty promises of weekly counseling, coaching calls, and post-adoption counseling after the baby was born. Again, assuming that the decision had already been made. Again, proving that she wasn't listening to me. As I heaved my belly up and we began walking to our respective cars, she got my attention once more. She announced that she'd almost forgotten to give me the large cardboard box of prospective parent profiles. She wanted me to go through them and let her know which options I liked.

My face was blank. I mentally shrieked at her to listen to my words even though I knew she wouldn't. There was no point in trying to say anything. She offered to put them in my car, but I shook my head and mutely took the box from her. I figured I could appease her and hasten my ability to exit the situation. Though I couldn't know for sure, part of me assumed that this would be the extent of the so-called counseling, coaching, and support.

I had my family's love, far away though they may have been, and God had placed some amazing people to provide additional support, but I knew it would all come down to me to choose: parenting or adoption. If I was going to parent, my first choice, I would have to start making the kinds of preparations all new parents make. Part of that was calculating the practical and financial aspects of making a baby work. I would have to get all of that in order, and I was running out of time. Nurse Patty had given me the advice about getting in touch with social services, and I decided to follow that advice. That included driving down to the financial aid office. It was a crazy concept for me; my entire life, I'd never been to a social service building of any kind. It was overwhelming, just like every other part of the pregnancy.

Prior to being pregnant, my mother had performed any task deemed "adult." I felt so young, walking in there, and awkward. The judgement was intense, though whether it was real or imagined hardly mattered. The woman at the reception window took one look at me and immediately asked what I was doing there. Nothing about "how can I help you?" I got the impression that she was really trying to tell me I didn't belong there.

"I have some questions. I don't know where to go. Is this the right place to ask questions?"

She told me to take a number and wait, not bothering to hide her staring at my distended belly. I cradled my stomach as I waited, unconsciously protective of my daughter under the judgmental gazes surrounding us. I held her close, reassuring both of us that I was doing the right thing. I kept thinking that we didn't belong there, that I deserved better, that she deserved better. I promised her and myself that it wouldn't be forever. It was just a start. I would finish high school and go to college. I'd ensure we had a good life.

My number came up and I was ushered into a small intake room. The intake agent asked if I had proof of pregnancy. I couldn't help but laugh aloud. He had to be joking! Wasn't my enormous belly and my newly acquired waddle proof enough? He remained stoic and informed me that once I could show proof of pregnancy, I would be eligible for food stamps and state medical insurance, all for free. All of his questions were delivered with the same blank monotone and no expression. It was very unsettling. He asked questions about where I lived, where my parents were, and had I been to the doctor. I tried to explain that because I was also considering adoption, the agency was currently paying for everything. I then shared that I wanted to learn more about what it would take to be a parent.

He interjected and strongly agreed that I should choose adoption. He commented that I was definitely too young to have a baby. Regardless of his social working knowledge, he didn't know me or my story. How I cried that fateful night in Montana for God to save her life. How, with every kick and movement, I bonded more and more with the beautiful baby growing inside of me. He couldn't know that when I stared uselessly at that ultrasound and found out that I carried a girl, tears had streamed down my cheeks. He was doing his job and I could respect that, but he had no way of knowing the impact of his words. I had no way of knowing that those words allowed me to take a large step towards real motherhood.

Some of my fears had been resolved; I was relieved to find there were financial resources available to us. I moved on to the next step, still struggling with the knowledge that I had sat in a financial aid office and therefore was unable to give my daughter everything she deserved. She was truly innocent in all of this and needed more than I could provide at that time. All the love in my heart was no substitute for financial stability. I wasn't ready to face that yet, though.

My next stop was a department store that specialized in babies. I brought a notepad and walked the aisles, pricing items and comparing brands. I tried to determine what was necessary and what wasn't. To predict how much of each thing I would need and how often I could afford to buy more. I tried to make a budget, even without the promise of income. I carefully recorded the prices for a stroller, a car seat, diapers, formula, a carrier, and bedding. I saw an adorable stuffed animal, the cutest elephant I'd ever seen. I had to buy it for her! I considered the price tag, $8.99, and the fact that it wasn't needed.

Sadly, I put the elephant back, reminding myself that I had to be more responsible now. As I did so, I saw another pregnant woman holding the hand of a small toddler. I watched as she held up a pair of pajamas, barely considered them, and threw them into her cart without thought. I didn't even see her check the price. Then she grabbed another and another. Three or four items went into the cart and she never once looked at the cost. I imagined how good that must feel. How much freedom would I have if money was not such a crucial issue? If I had that money, could I keep my baby?

Once she left, I surreptitiously wandered over to the clothes she'd been adding and checked the prices myself. I realized that I didn't even have enough money to buy the clothes, let alone all of the other things a baby would need. Babies are expensive! I hadn't processed just how costly their supplies were, and this was a rude wake-up call. That feeling of being overwhelmed threatened me once more. How could I do this?

That night, I chronicled the day's events in my journal. I wrote to my daughter how I wanted to give her the world. I wanted to buy her everything she needed and more besides. Everything like dolls, toys, clothes, whatever a little girl's heart desired. I told her: right now, I do not know how I'll do this, but I promise, I will figure it out. Paralyzed by an overwhelming sense of lacking finances and maturity, I couldn't rationalize keeping her. I couldn't imagine how I could take care of her, the way she so richly deserved.

The next morning, when I arrived at school, my feet knew exactly where to go. The one person who had always been available, any time I needed her. I went straight to visit Nurse Patty. I shared my financial research with her, my pricing, and my lackluster conclusions. Unexpectedly, I began crying when I got to the part about putting back the stuffed elephant, when I longed to be the other mother. I explained how hard it was to find out about food stamps, insurance, and welfare. She listened to me go on and on until I finally ran out of both tears and words.

"And how did that make you feel?"

Cliché though the words may be, they cut to the heart of the issue. In some ways, it sparked a good feeling, because knowledge is power and knowing more meant that I had more of an understanding of what it would take to raise my daughter myself. There was still a little hope. I admitted, with a heavy heart, that though I was capable of parenting, I knew my daughter deserved more. None of this was fair to anyone involved. Nurse Patty took my hand, as she had many times before, and calmly advised me:

"Whatever decision you make, have no regret."

In that moment, without hesitation or contemplation, I knew that once I had made my choice, I would never look back. Whether I chose parenting or adoption, I would honor her words. I would not regret. Regret would never be a part of whatever choice I made.

Despite the reassurance, I still had a lot to think about. As I left her office and returned to my classes, I spent the day with my thoughts racing, chasing each other in circles. The journal was essential, both to remember the important things I learned and because it was all too much to keep inside my head. I had to get everything on to paper. I hoped that writing them down would help me organize the intense mixture of emotions, fears, and hopes and separate those from the facts. Just as I was writing, the phone rang. My father was calling. I always recognized his voice immediately, but he often felt the need to announce "It's Dad!" I was overjoyed to hear from him; usually my mom was the one who called. I crossed my fingers that everything was okay.

"What's up?"

"Nothing. What're you doing?"

A wave of relief washed over me and I relaxed a little. We ended up talking for a few minutes, not about anything in particular. Just hearing his voice was enough. The connection, the love and warmth he radiated through the phone, was enough to bring me peace. It was inexplicable, but knowing that he loved me, missed me, just as much as I missed him was such a relief. When it was time to hang up, he reminded me that he loved me. I knew it, of course, but I enjoyed hearing it aloud. I returned the sentiment and went back to journaling.

I realized, possibly for the first time, that if I chose to raise my baby, it was likely that she might never have such a loving father. My father's love had always been a pillar of strength in my life. He'd taught me so many useful things: how to ride a bike, change a flat tire, and check the oil level in my car. We had traditions, he and I, that were completely unique to us. Stricken with grief, I gripped my pen tightly. Of all the things I knew I couldn't give my daughter, it hadn't occurred to me that I wouldn't even be able to provide something I'd always taken for granted.

I tried to reason that she'd share my father; he would be her grandfather and there was no reason that they couldn't be just as close as he was with me, but I knew it wouldn't be the same. Being fatherless was not what I wanted for my daughter. All the love I had wouldn't be enough to make up for not having a dad. I hadn't settled on an answer, but it was a new fear to contend with and something I had to consider very carefully. I held on to the conversation I'd had with Nurse Patty and knew, more than ever, that, in order to make sure I would have no regrets, I needed as much information as I could gather. My time was running short and I had to make a choice. Not a choice for my parents, my church, my friends, or even for me. I had to make my daughter's choice, long before she took her first breath.

# SIX

# *Undefined by "Birth Mom"*

*"Then the woman whose son was living spoke to the king, for she yearned*
*with compassion for her son; and she said, "O my lord, give her the living*
*child, and by no means kill him!""*
*(1 Kings 3:26)*

I remembered the box of binders, days after the meeting with the adoption agency, still sitting on my passenger seat. I hadn't looked through them. Why would I need to? They represented a choice that I wasn't ready to make. Yet, that night, I knew the mature thing to do would be to properly consider all of my options. I had been selfish before, only thinking about what I wanted. But being a mom would have to mean putting her needs ahead of mine, no matter how difficult.

After reassuring my surrogate family that I just needed something from my car, I retrieved the box of records from where it had been staring at me for the past few days. I hadn't so much as looked inside; I knew what it held. It represented my homecoming from the hospital with no baby in my arms. It held the names of strangers, strangers who wanted my baby. The potential for my baby's future that didn't hold me. I awkwardly made my way back inside the house, the box surprisingly heavy. I had just finished climbing back into my temporary bed when I was interrupted by Shelly and Tony's three-year-old son, Jeffrey. He wanted me to read to him. It had become our tradition every night, since the second week. I finished the story and closed the book with a satisfactory snap and, with a hug, he went on his way. The story and hug fortified me to finally open the box, though I did so with trepidation.

There must have been around ten binders inside, all containing information that threatened my future as a mom. I opened the first one cautiously, surprised to see pictures of a family, smiling at me from the front page. These were real people with actual, real lives, not my imagination conjuring whatever scary adoptive parents it wanted. It was all suddenly too real, too much to process. It would have to wait until I was in a better head space.

I cried myself to sleep that night, uncertain and afraid, cradling my belly as I drifted off. The next morning, beams of sun filtered through my window. Refreshed, I took a quick trip to the bathroom and determined to try again with the binders. Shelly popped her head in to ask if I wanted eggs for breakfast, but I told her I'd eat later. She was very sweet to me, considering that we'd never met before all of this. She saw the binders I'd seized, spread out all over the bed and how vigorously I pored through them.

"Are those all the potential parents?"

"There's a lot of people who need babies. But I've only got one!"

I smiled, albeit half-heartedly.

"God will help guide you."

Distracted, I thanked her once more as she closed the door. This time, I opened them one at a time, trying not to overwhelm myself. I investigated their pictures, their profiles, and their letters. I scoured all of the available information, but I found the letters to be the most telling. Each prospective family wrote a letter addressed to the birth mom. I'd never heard the term "birth mom" and, at the time, I didn't care much for it. Something about the term implied a temporary situation that unsettled me, but over time I would come to embrace it. I still hadn't given up on parenting entirely, but I wanted my research to be well-thought out and logically reasoned. I read the letters again and again as I scanned the respective pictures. I thought, if I looked hard enough, maybe I could see into their souls. One after another. It was almost too much just to see the sheer quantity of people who wanted babies, who already keenly felt love for a baby they hadn't yet met.

Despite all that, I only had one baby to give. I couldn't appease them all. And I also wondered how so many of them could claim to love me, the birth mom, and my baby, when they knew nothing about us—had never even heard my name. I began separating people I had eliminated from the "maybe" pile. My criteria were crude and juvenile, but I didn't know any better. If I didn't like the picture, or if I thought they sounded stuffy and boring...in retrospect, it probably wasn't fair how many of them I eliminated for ultimately stupid reasons. I finally narrowed it down to two potential couples. I couldn't help but wonder about them, though. As much as they wanted a child and claimed to love it, as much as they said they'd always wanted a baby—well I'm the same. I'd always wanted to be a mom too! I wanted this baby. I loved her and she was mine. I put the binders away as thoughts for another time.

In the days that followed, I'd spend a lot of time re-reading the letters and imprinting the pictures of the two prospective families in my mind. They already seemed almost familiar. I still had so many questions, so many worries. One of my biggest fears in choosing adoption was the looming anxiety that my daughter might feel unwanted. She might suspect that I gave her away from lack of love. What if she didn't feel valued? Truly, she had become the most important person in my life, and I couldn't stand the thought that she might not know just how special she is. If she thought that I had abandoned her... I would be heartbroken.

Was there some way to choose adoption, but still let her know why I had to, how much I cherished our time together during pregnancy, and how much I loved her? Would the adoptive parents tell her how much I cared? Maybe they wouldn't even know! How much interaction would I be allowed? Could I communicate directly with them, after the adoption, or would it all have to go through the agency? I'd already seen how the agency treated its so-called promises, and I knew I couldn't rely on only their word that the adoptive parents would know my intentions. Without that crucial discussion, they might think I was simply a stupid, young girl who didn't want her baby. That couldn't be farther from the truth, and I had to convey that.

I wanted to keep her more than anything. I wanted to have the chance to really be her mom, more than I cared about pleasing anyone else. I was terrified to stand up to the agency and my parents, but I knew that I could. I could do it for her. Nothing would ever change that. Whether I was called a "birth mom" or not, I was her mother. She certainly had changed me by being my daughter. I was changed for the better. Though not defined by rape or promiscuity, I would always be defined by the choices I made for her. The life I chose for us. No matter what happened, I desperately wanted her to look back and be proud of her mother. I have always wanted that, and still do.

In my mind, the rape was only a catalyst, and was entirely unconnected from the beautiful angel growing inside of me. Some people have difficulty separating the event from the result, which is completely understandable, but I was able to compartmentalize. I adored her! She was the best thing that had ever happened to me in my short life. This baby had nothing to do with that man. According to the paperwork of the adoption agency, Jason was the father. There would be no mention of the boorish thug who'd taken advantage of me, nor should there be. Any man can have a child, but he had no claim on her. He had no right to be called her father. She was the pinnacle of my life and he had no place there. I spent the day in quiet contemplation of her, slowly rubbing small circles over my swollen stomach.

Earlier that week, my mom and I had agreed that I could come home for a short visit. I planned to leave Friday, after school, and stay for the weekend. I was so excited! I had barely seen my family the past few months and I missed them terribly. I missed my room, my own bed, eating in our kitchen, and relaxing on our couch. Seeing my family meant being surrounded by my loving support system. I remembered the feeling of wanting to escape so badly from that house. Those memories already seemed to have faded, and I wondered what I could possibly have been thinking. Home was a refuge again.

Before heading to school that day, I laboriously packed my bags for the weekend. I was on edge, impatiently waiting for the last bell to ring. No time would be wasted. My dad had reminded me to check the oil in my car prior to the trip, and I'd already taken care of it. I was fully gassed up and ready to go! I'd already begun to pack up before the bell even rang, knowing that I was incapable of actually rushing anywhere. I made a quick pit stop for sunflower seeds and a drink and then I was on the road. A three-hour drive was not exactly appealing, in my state, but I was more than willing to make the sacrifice.

I still knew the way, even with the time that had passed; I just had to stay to the left on the freeway and it would eventually take me home. The long drive was peaceful, but that only gave me more time to consider my daughter. I had so much more knowledge, but every bit of research I'd done only made the situation more tangible. In the absence of my family and close friends, I was forced to make a life-changing decision.

I wouldn't make it that day—no, that weekend was for rest and relaxation with my family. I idly began munching on the sunflower seeds before realizing that I had nothing to use as a trash bag. I shrugged my shoulders and tossed the seeds on the plastic mats of my passenger floor, figuring I would throw them away and clean up when I got home. As I popped the seeds into my mouth, one by one, interspersed with regular sips of my Coke, I lost track of time. I did not know the strain of the psychological stress on my body. It only felt like mere moments and I had somehow teleported over 120 miles! When I came back to myself, I was suddenly aware of a sign announcing that my home was only thirty miles away. I sat up straighter and glanced around, completely confused. It had to be wrong! I was just in Los Angeles!

Out of the corner of my eye, I noticed the floor, littered with hundreds of seeds. It was then that I realized how deeply I had zoned out. It was a little worrying. I was really glad I hadn't crashed or gone off onto the shoulder. And yet, the weight on my shoulders felt a little bit lighter. In the midst of my confusion and worry that I might be losing my mind, the driving trance I'd been in gave me a real sense of peace. Suddenly, everything was crystal clear.

I loved my daughter with every fiber of my being. She was inextricably linked with me, and nothing could sever that bond. She deserved so much more than I, a jobless sixteen-year-old whose family barely managed financially, could offer her. Those families could give her more. A mom and a dad, a stable environment, and either one parent or nanny who would always be home with her. I'd have to spend my days going to school or work and she would need constant care and attention. Not to mention, all the toys, clothes, and necessities I couldn't afford. The only way to show her just how much I loved her was to let go. This option, which had been so obvious to everyone else, right from the beginning, only dawned on me then, while I fretted over losing concentration during a drive. There was no more second-guessing to be done. Instead, there was only overwhelming relief and hope. Joy enveloped me and I knew I felt it for her, for the amazing life I would give her.

When I pulled up in front of my house, my brother was waiting outside. I was so happy to see him! He shot me a welcoming smile and teased me about my huge belly. I rolled my eyes in return. Neither of us needed to say it aloud. We had really missed each other. He alone shared my childhood. Likely, he was the only person who understood the difficulties involved in defying our parents or disappointing them. I did feel bad that my circumstances had taken up so much of the spotlight. I hoped he wouldn't resent me for it. We knew that we would eventually be each other's only family when we got older and our parents aged and someday passed on. We'd be the ones responsible for keeping the family stories and traditions alive.

That wonderful weekend mainly consisted of a jumble of my mother's famous tacos, her delicious chicken and dumplings, and a few short, special walks with my father. It was exactly the respite I had needed, an oasis of happiness. I was refreshed and clear-headed when I returned to my temporary home. My daughter and I had such hope for the future. Now that I had finally come to a conclusion, I was almost light-headed and giddy planning ahead. Maybe she would have siblings in the future! For sure, at least, she'd have a mom and dad. She'd have a home. As I imagined the lives she could have, I knew I still had one more important decision to make: choosing her parents.

When I arrived back at Shelly and Tony's, they welcomed me with smiles. Shelly had saved me some dinner, and Tony offered to help me unload the car since they knew I'd be hungry. They'd become familiar to me now and I grinned, happy to see them and read to Jeffrey again. As I climbed into bed, the two profiles I'd narrowed down in hands, I began the real work. I recognized that I would be changing one couple's lives forever and the three of us would always share a special bond, in the form of our daughter. I had no doubts that they'd love her; who wouldn't? But would they love me? Would they allow me, in some capacity, to be a part of my daughter's life? I laid down and considered the portfolios again, drawn to both couples for different reasons.

One couple, Lisa and James, were young and attractive. They'd already been married for eight years and were excited to choose adoption after struggling for years with infertility. On the other hand, there were Frank and Kelly. They were obviously deeply in love with each other, though less attractive than Lisa and James. I worried that Frank and Kelly would have more trouble connecting with a teen mother through their letters and picture than Lisa and James, not for any failings on their part, but because Lisa and James came across as very charismatic and beautiful. Any girl would choose them, surely! I felt drawn to Frank and Kelly because I thought they were the less obvious choice and prided myself on not being as shallow as other teenage girls. Kelly's maternal figure was a soft reminder of my own mother and I thought about all of the times I had been engulfed in her arms. I wanted that for my daughter too.

I pulled out the letters to read again with new eyes—with the intention, this time, of really choosing my daughter's family. My new family too, hopefully. I started again with Frank and Kelly. They were very sweet, and I tried to imagine how they would react to the news that they'd been chosen to receive a baby girl. I smiled, thinking about how much joy I could give them. Then, to be fair, I picked up the other profile. For the first time, when I scanned James' letter, I heard it in what I assumed his voice sounded like. A father's voice, of love and hope, of protection and godliness. Truly, the father my daughter deserved. Tears pricked my eyes and began to roll down my face as I read on.

My name is James. My wife, Lisa, and I have prayed for you over the last year. I can only imagine, at this time, what you are going through. For us, it has been a time of building anticipation, waiting patiently, and trusting. I can only admire your courage to give your child up for adoption. For the last seven and a half years, Lisa and I have tried, unsuccessfully, to have children of our own. Due to Lisa's many surgeries, we had to look for another way. To be honest with you, I am so glad we did. Lisa and I have spent the last two years preparing for this child. To make sure he/she is welcomed into a safe and secure home. We now know how blessed we are to accept this child into our family. We want you to know that God's hand is upon you at this time. We trust that you are being guided by His peace in your heart towards the best decision for your child. You will always hold a special place, in our hearts and minds. Love, James

Even more than the physical words on the page, I could hear his sensitivity and his love. For his wife, for God, and for his future child. I knew instinctively that he could be the father my daughter needed—her protector, her rock—just as my dad was for me. James could demonstrate how a man should follow God and love his family. Lisa's letter, by comparison, was shorter, but I could imagine how it felt. This beautiful young woman, sitting down to write the letter. The vulnerability and uncertainty she conveyed pierced my heart.

... I believe adoption is the highest act of giving that exists. We will always be grateful for the opportunity you've given us. You'll always be in our hearts and prayers, as you already have been. Love, Lisa

After reading those letters, I fell asleep that night with the peace James had spoken of settling over me like a warm blanket. Like I was covered in God's presence. These two people, once strangers, now felt like the most important people in my life, after my baby. I had already begun the journey of falling in love with them and the depths of their affections. A journey that now, 31 years later, still hasn't ended.

I had six more weeks to truly prepare myself for the birth. I knew it would be the hardest day of my life; nobody had ever promised that it would be easy. I never thought it would be. I had thought by making the decision to give her up for adoption, I had surmounted the last hurdle, but I realized that my job was far from over. I had lots of preparation left for the adoption to go through and also for my own well-being. I was absolutely not ready to go into labor; I hadn't even considered the reality that the perfect baby growing inside of me would, eventually, need to come out. Shelly assured me that I didn't need to take Lamaze classes because she would be my labor coach and would never leave my side. Gratitude swelled up once more for this nurse who had taken me in and was such a steady presence in my time of need.

I recognized that I needed to be prepared for a time when my daughter would no longer be with me. We had been together for nearly a whole year, sixteen now forever marked in my mind as a life-altering year. I tried to imagine life without my baby, attempting to pretend I wasn't pregnant anymore and straining to remember a time before I'd ever conceived all of this. I made a real effort to assess my heart and mind.

One day, as I was doing the laundry, I pretended I'd already given birth. She wasn't with me. What would I be thinking about? If my baby wasn't constantly occupying my thoughts, what would? Would I think about what she was doing? I'd probably think about whether she was sleeping or eating or crying...whether she was at the grocery store in her stroller, cautiously observing her surroundings like many babies do. I did my best to prepare for the separation. I started pretending she was already gone on a regular basis, to shore up my resolve for the actual event. At first, I was only able to pretend for a moment or two. I'd have to drop the act and grab my belly, reassuring myself that, at least for now, she was still there. Not gone yet. I wasn't ready, I couldn't let her go. Not right then. But, it got easier and easier each time and I knew it was the healthy thing to do for myself.

In a way, it was grieving, but it wasn't really. I had to ready myself for a life without her constant presence, but one in which I would know she was out there, somewhere. Living, being loved, breathing, walking, talking, and becoming the person she was destined to be. Just, doing it without me. I knew that in the future, when I had more children, (because I always knew I would), I would never be ashamed to tell others about my first daughter. I would hold my head high when I joyfully gushed about her to others because I was proud to be her mom. There was no room in my heart for regret, not when it was filled to bursting with such love.

My someday children would never be sat down and told, in hushed tones, about some shameful tale from my deep, dark past. This girl would be part of our everyday lives, someone they always knew about. A big sister they could love and look up to.

To hide what happened would dishonor my daughter, and I refused to cover her up like a dirty secret. There was nothing dirty about the miracle in my womb, nothing violent, nothing horrible. The ways in which she'd forced me to change and mature were integral to my personality, and I was happy to explain them. This wasn't the end; it was only the beginning, and I would treat it as such. Letting go of her didn't mean I had to let her go.

I had picked out an amazing couple to hold her when I could not. A mom and dad who would raise her in a similar home to the one I'd grown up in. To the one I would continue growing up in. She'd be taught the same morals, the same values, and would hold the same beliefs. I had wanted to find a Christian family because God had been such a forceful presence in my life, and in hers, already!

Once more, it was time to contact the adoption agency. They had already broken promises to me and failed to fulfill their end of the bargain, but, in the end, it didn't matter. They gave me access to two people I believed were sent by God to love and care for my daughter. It didn't matter to me how I'd gotten there, only that I was there. The "why"s and "how"s of the agency failing me weren't important. Regardless of the failings of man, God had provided a way. He gave me Lisa and James. Together, this triad of us would bond over a gorgeous little girl and would do everything in our power to give her the best life possible. We would share our love and appreciation for her with each other. I called and asked to speak to Brenda.

I tried to start the conversation, not waiting for her to fill the line with idle chit-chat. Unfortunately, she interrupted me immediately to ask if I'd chosen the parents for the baby. Her words rankled. "The" baby? Not "your" baby? Not to mention, Brenda knew she was a girl, but still said "the baby" as if it was some vague concept. It felt like an annoying strategy to help me detach from the process and from my daughter. I took a breath and didn't let it faze me.

"I think so, but I have some questions about Lisa and James."

She twittered that I should be so happy, I had made the perfect choice, "oh they were so great." I cut her off to explain my need for an open adoption. I knew times had changed from my parents' generation and these days, people could have a unique relationship, even when they weren't directly raising a child. I wanted to receive letters and pictures. To invite them to my wedding one day. To be invited to their special events over the years. I knew what I needed to facilitate my healing. I couldn't imagine a life spent not knowing what my daughter looked like! I couldn't think of walking through a mall and wondering if that baby, that toddler, that teenager, that woman was my daughter. I wanted to be involved in her life, and I wanted her in mine. I wanted to be able to extend the affection I felt to that couple and embrace them wholeheartedly. Brenda acknowledged my feelings and said that Lisa and James felt the same, that we all wanted an open adoption.

They would be her parents and we all understood that, but they also wanted me in their lives. That finally brought the reassurance that I'd been searching for the entire pregnancy. The certainty that I had made the right choice. Brenda wanted to know why I'd chosen them in particular, but I didn't feel comfortable sharing the sincere connection I'd developed from their letters and how God had guided me. I couldn't put into words what I felt for Lisa, the woman who would take over my role as mother, who would get to love and nurture my daughter. Who, I felt, was essentially replacing me.

I knew she had loving arms that could gently comfort my daughter when she needed it. A mom who would teach her about life and give her the tools to be a strong, godly woman herself one day. I trusted her to do that. I trusted God's control. I simply told Brenda that I felt like Lisa and James loved each other. Their life was already complete without a child, but that a baby would bring them more. That they were already fulfilled with each other and with God, but my daughter would be an additional joy. I truly felt their prayers through the letters and how much they loved me, despite not knowing who I was.

The agency agreed to set up a meeting between the three of us the following week. They wanted me to meet them, to confirm my decision. So that I could know it was really the right family. I told them my decision had already been made. That no meeting would change my mind. My daughter was their daughter too. Of course I wanted to meet them! But not in an interview setting, not while they were still in doubt of my choice. My hope was that we could begin building a relationship together.

However, that meeting would never happen because, far ahead of my schedule, I began having contractions.

# SEVEN

# *Undefined by Stolen Moments*

*"Be anxious for nothing, but in everything by prayer and supplication,*
*with thanksgiving, let your requests be made known to God"*
*(Philippians 4:6)*

It was around eleven at night; I was in bed trying to get some rest. I started experiencing some abdominal pain, but I sleepily brushed it off as normal kicks and movement. I didn't know what was happening. Even as I rolled over and tried to fall asleep once more, the pains continued. I wasn't ignorant; Shelly had explained to me what contractions felt like and the entire labor process, from beginning to end. I didn't recognize the contractions for what they were until I noticed that they were happening rhythmically and intensifying. I desperately hoped that I wasn't going into labor. I didn't want it to be over; I wasn't ready to say goodbye yet. Every time the pain wracked my body, I was one step closer to letting my daughter go.

When it finally became obvious that I could no longer ignore the pain, I went to wake Shelly up. I was somewhat embarrassed to walk into the master bedroom, to impose on her in the middle of the night. What if I was wrong? I might be waking her up for no real reason. I tapped her and she quickly awoke, following me softly back into my room. She asked me to lay down so that she could put her hands on my belly and see if they really were contractions and to see how consistent they were. She began timing them with a nurse's practiced hands. She quickly confirmed that they were, in fact, contractions, and we should begin heading to the hospital.

I rushed to pack a bag; I hadn't done so yet because I supposedly still had eleven days to go. As I picked up my stuff I realized my bag and I will come back, but my baby will not. I cradled my belly once more, memorizing how it felt to have her inside of me. I tried to call my parents, but there was no answer. Likely, they'd gone to sleep as it was nearing midnight. Shelly drove us thirty minutes to the hospital, and I assumed she'd called the doctor ahead of time. I asked her to try reaching my parents again, and she reassured me that, once we were settled, she would do so. As the pain increased, all I could think was that it was too soon, I wasn't ready, too soon! I was more panicked about the implications than the actual pain.

That day had begun like any other Wednesday. I went to school, and, only a few hours before the contractions began, I'd been spending time with my new friends at church youth group, the one JJ had introduced me to. We'd hung out like a bunch of normal teenagers and yet now I was on the way to the hospital to give birth. It all happened so fast! With each new round of pain, time with my precious little girl was running out. Of course, I wanted to see her, to hold her. I couldn't wait to do that, but, at the same time, I could wait. Labor was the beginning of the end. How would I be able to say goodbye? I'd only just begun rehearsing my farewells. I wondered if I would be strong enough to make it. Terrified that the answer was no. Shelly glanced over at me and I could feel the concern brimming.

"How're you doing?"

Maybe she knew I was struggling. Perhaps she thought I was afraid of the pain. I was not. Physically, I was ready to take on this labor. Mentally though...I knew there was no way to put the grieving loss I already felt into words so I tried to respond casually, taking a few deep breaths. The strain was still audible.

"Yep, I'm good."

When we finally arrived, it seemed like everyone had known we were coming. I could hear people whispering, but I didn't care. Shelly and the doctors started discussing my options and making the medical decisions that my parents had entrusted to her with my care. Everything I heard sounded like technical jargon. They had me change out of my clothes into a hospital gown and gave me an IV. They kept talking about labor as a natural process, trying to soothe and calm me. None of them understood the situation. They didn't get it. I was about to give this life, my baby, to someone else, and here they were, talking about how long to expect and the levels of pain. Like that mattered! I tried to focus on remembering every detail. I would never forget any of it. Even now, having had five additional children who I took home with me afterwards, that first labor is etched deep into my soul. Labor didn't mean the same things to me that it does for most people. Labor would not bring my daughter into my arms. Instead, it would be the onset of her journey out of them.

Hours passed. Shelly had instructed the doctor to give me an epidural, so I wasn't feeling any pains anymore. I remember her saying to the doctor that "a person who is not going to have a baby should never have to experience the pain of having one." Her comment confused me at the time; I just figured that she didn't understand. How could she? She'd never given a child away. Jeffrey was three, and she'd been able to have those precious three years with him. I wanted to experience the pain. Maybe I wanted to have something to hold onto when I didn't have her. I just wanted it to be real. Muffling it with medicine seemed to suppress the actuality of giving birth, but the decision, like many before it, was made without consulting me.

The labor pains subsided. The nurses would let me know when I was having a contraction, but I couldn't feel it. Somehow, I thought it wasn't fair. I wanted to have the full experience of childbirth, especially since I wouldn't be taking my baby home. Before I could dwell on it too hard, they told me it was time to push. I couldn't wait to see her face! She was going to be so beautiful. I was so excited to hold her. The nurses told me to give a couple of practice pushes while the doctor was on his way. As soon as I tried, someone yelled for me to stop. I heard someone else say:

"The baby's going to come out the next time she pushes!"

They instructed me to stop pushing, to buy some time for the doctor to arrive. More people entered the room. I lay there on the bed, helplessly exposed and vulnerable. Nurses bustled around the room in preparation for the birth. I just looked around, soaking in the situation, storing every shred of this memory. Without explaining anything, I was abruptly wheeled out of the room. I didn't know why or where I was going. It didn't bother me. I just laid back and allowed the medical professionals to do their jobs.

I remained convinced that I was the only person who realized what a momentous occasion this truly was. A little girl, born of one mother, bound to live with another. As I was rolled into a small, sterile room, I figured it was likely the delivery room. I noticed a small baby bed with clear sides. I knew it wouldn't be long until my baby was laying in it. My baby.

Immediately, I began to panic. My baby! This is my baby! I can't go through with the adoption! I have to keep her; I will keep her. I'll figure something out! All the months of planning, journaling, and determination were washed away in that single moment. I couldn't fathom letting her go. As the doctor finally walked in, I told him:

"I want to keep my baby."

He looked up from the foot of my bed. Even around his surgical mask, I could see a gentle smile.

"It's not too late; it's still your choice. But right now, I need you to push."

His words brought me immense relief. It wasn't too late! Praise God, it's not too late! The next contraction happened naturally and I hardly had to help it along. My daughter was born at 7:41 a.m. The doctor announced that it was a girl. It wasn't a surprise, but the moment was still magical. If it was possible, I loved her even more than ever before. He held her up so I could see. My eyes fixed on her tiny body. Her cries echoed throughout the room. She was perfect. Her skin was as white as snow.

"I want to keep her."

I announced again, thoughtlessly reaching my arms out for this new, naked, wet baby. He assured me that I could hold her soon, but not yet. That I'd have to be patient while he cut the umbilical cord. Suddenly, it felt like I was caught in slow motion. Slowly, the scissors moved to sever the tissue connecting me and my daughter. The cord dropped soundlessly in the silent room. She was released from my body. In that split second, I was overwhelmed with the realization that my time as her mother was over. By the time he finally handed me that precious bundle, I was holding James and Lisa's baby. He placed her into my arms and I keenly felt the bond between us. I loved her so much! I had cared for her for so long already and I knew

I'd never stop. Now was our time. I knew it would be brief, but I'd cherish every moment.

As she laid on my chest, I thought about what her name would be. It wasn't fair that she didn't yet have one. I'd liked the names Sarah or Ashley, but I didn't give her one. It wasn't mine to choose. I prayed for her future, just as I had many times in the past. I prayed to God to watch over my sweet angel. To keep her safe and healthy. That she would live a life full of joy and love. That she would learn to love Him as much as I did and to serve Him all of her life. I asked Him to help her understand just how much I loved her. An insight that went beyond any reason, a gift imparted from Him. That He would help her understand why I chose adoption. I also prayed that James and Lisa would embrace her seamlessly into their lives. I thanked God for bringing my daughter into my life and for helping me thus far. I knew I'd continue to need His help in the coming years.

Not long after, I began to feel nauseated, and the nurses took my baby away. They promised to bring her back after she'd been bathed. An onslaught of panic rushed over me, that she was leaving. I'd been preparing for it, but I still wasn't ready. The nurse must have noticed because she looked down at me and reiterated that they would bring her back. Relief chased away the panic. I didn't have to say goodbye just yet. I laid in the recovery room after they took her out. I wanted out myself. I wanted to be back with her! I'd been waiting so long to meet her. It was our turn to be together in person, our time. This is all we would have. Every minute without her was a minute lost forever.

Discomfort spread throughout my body. I hated it. They tried telling me that I needed to rest, to recover my strength. Anger surged through me. I'm strong now! I can sleep later! I needed to see my baby now! I pleaded several times for them to bring her back, but they insisted that I wait.

126

I had heard nothing about my parents. I wondered if they would come. Shelly must have gone home at some point because I was utterly alone. A few hours went by, and I was wheeled into a different room again. On the way, they assured me that I could have my baby back. Was Shelly calling the adoption agency? They'd certainly need to be alerted. James and Lisa didn't even know that I had planned to meet them; that I had chosen them. I thought about them a lot during those hours alone. I wondered what they'd be doing when they got the news. Would Lisa pick up the phone when the agency called, or would she later listen to the voicemail? What would she be feeling? Nerves, anxiety? Would James be home or at work? Who would hear the news first? How will they celebrate? I imagined them staying up all night in each other's arms, torn between worry and excitement. I knew, in their place, I'd be anxious. They had no way of knowing if I might change my mind at the last minute, the way I almost had. I would never do that to them. To my daughter.

While I waited to hear something, or for someone to come in, those types of anxieties began bubbling up. My daughter had been gone for too long. I started to piece together that this might be a strategy to prevent me from changing my mind about the adoption, that I might be bonding too closely with her. It was far too late for that. I pushed the call button again and demanded that someone allow me to see my daughter. I felt a little bad about my tone, but I couldn't stop the frustration from bleeding into my voice. I wanted someone to listen! That time, my demand was heard. A few minutes later, a clean bundle of joy rolled into the room. Her hair was soft and fluffy, her cheeks rosy. I breathed a sigh of relief. She was swaddled up to look like a burrito, her beautiful face poking out the top with curious blue eyes. I thought again that she was perfect.

A gift of love and promise: Locket Given, "Love, James and Lisa"

The first thing I did was to unwrap the carefully folded blanket. I had to see her, this life I'd created. I counted all of her fingers and toes. I've never been able to reconcile the innate, maternal fear of babies having extra fingers and toes, but it seems to be a fact of life. Luckily, she had the right numbers. I stared at her eyelashes, trying to memorize her sweet face. I gently traced her translucent eyebrows with a finger. She momentarily flashed those baby blues my way, but softly closed them once more. I figured she was exhausted from recent events. I spoke to her gently. Whenever I'd speak, she attempted to open her eyes again. Maybe she recognized my voice? But the battle against sleep was futile. I couldn't believe all of that had been inside of me for so long. Such beauty! She was finally real and in my arms.

I couldn't wait to share her with James and Lisa! I was so proud of this beautiful life that I had cared for. I'd made sure to eat well, take vitamins, everything recommended during pregnancy. I knew that the minute they saw her, they would love her as their own. I took pride in those moments, while I fed her and spoke words incomprehensible to her new ears. I spoke to that infant, but my words were meant for the woman she would become one day. I prayed that, in time, she would be driven to find me, no matter how far apart we ended up. That our connection would last a lifetime. I needn't have worried.

Soon, the nurse came back, insisting that she needed to, once again, take my baby away. I told her that I was fine. It was no problem. I wanted to be with her, but my words fell on deaf ears. There was no reason to take her. When I asked, the nurse dodged the question and reiterated how much I needed to rest, but I knew it was a ploy to stop me from spending time with my daughter. I tried to resist, but ultimately, the nurse won out by sheer force of will. Again, they robbed me of my already short time.

Frustrated and unable to rest, I called Brenda. She excitedly told me how she'd only just delivered the good news to Lisa. It was actually the second time she'd reached out to Lisa; the first was a few days prior when she had asked them the questions I'd had. She'd been sure to keep the questions broad so that they wouldn't know that a potential birth mom was considering them for placement. This time, when Lisa had picked up she'd told Brenda, only half-joking, that she shouldn't call unless there was a baby because every time she called, it gave them hope. Brenda had replied that Lisa shouldn't get too excited...it was only a baby girl! I couldn't know then that Lisa had been out gardening that day, or how she'd been humming a song in anticipation. All I knew, beyond a shadow of a doubt, was that Lisa must have been thrilled. Brenda had told Lisa that they could meet me and the baby the next day. I was exhilarated just listening to the story! It was really important to me that I have as many details as possible. But, the best was yet to come.

Brenda then shared that Lisa and James had picked out two names and wanted me to choose between them. I couldn't believe it! This was such a special privilege; one I hadn't allowed myself to want. I was elated that they'd already picked out names, maybe lying in bed one night, discussing the symbolism behind them or if they were family names. More than that, they wanted me to pick. I waited with bated breath to hear my choices: Rose and Sarah. I'm sure I gasped. I had loved the name Sarah forever; how many times had I doodled it in my journal now? I didn't need any time to ponder, once I'd swallowed the thickness in my throat, I croaked out:

"Sarah. It's Sarah. She's Sarah!"

I said it over and over, basking in the sound of her name. Any doubts I may have still harbored were erased. Sarah was my daughter, their daughter. Our daughter. After I hung up, I spent more time imagining how Lisa was feeling. I loved that I'd given this woman, virtually a stranger, such joy. I tried to picture how she'd tell her husband that their prayers had finally been answered. Fulfillment seeped through my soul at being able to give this couple their greatest gift. I loved them long before I knew them.

A few hours later, my own parents arrived. I knew it was hard for them to meet their first grandchild, knowing that they wouldn't be able to watch her grow up. That she wouldn't remember them. I knew they were also worried about me, their own daughter, who'd been forced to grow up so fast. I told them that Sarah was in the nursery, and they could go hold her. I did have an ulterior motive; I wanted them to tell the nurses to bring her back in my room. I thought the nurse might listen to my parents, even if they persisted in ignoring me.

When they came back, my dad was chuckling.

"Sarah is the youngest baby I've ever held!"

He told the story our family knew so well about how he couldn't be in the delivery room when I was born and couldn't hold me until I came home from the hospital. Behind the smiles and nostalgia, though, his worry was palpable. For me and my future. My mom, very much the same, complimented Sarah's beauty, but her focus was squarely on me. They didn't stay long that day and, in hindsight, I realize how difficult an ordeal it was for them.

It was my only day to share alone with Sarah. Although the lack of sleep from the night before had started catching up with me, I was determined that sleep would wait. The following day, Sarah would meet her parents and begin bonding with the mom who would hold her for the rest of her life. Today, what was left of it anyway, was mine.

Everyone left and I was alone again. Aggressively, I asked for Sarah to be brought to me. The nurse agreed, but then gave me an excuse about Sarah currently being fed and that she'd be brought in after the feeding. I wouldn't allow any more excuses! I firmly stated that I wanted to be the one to feed her. I wanted to hold her. In the face of my stubbornness, the nurse sighed and finally revealed the real reason the staff had all been so cagey about giving me time with Sarah.

"Sweetie, the more you're with her, the harder this will be."

I couldn't believe her naivety. It couldn't get any harder. I knew I was holding James and Lisa's daughter, but it was still my time with her. I wanted that, more than anything. Eventually, the nurse saw I could not be swayed and brought Sarah back. I never really had what should have been mine: a day with my daughter. I made the most of our short hours; telling her about how much God and I loved her, of His protection and grace. I believe that God gives parents the authority to bestow those great blessings upon their children and I did my best to convey them to Sarah. It was my privilege and responsibility, and I cherished that day. It was my moment to be a mom. Sarah laid with me for hours, sleeping peacefully while I watched.

Eventually, night fell. My body, exhausted from lack of sleep, labor, the adrenaline, and emotion from the day, could not fight sleep any longer. I called a nurse to take Sarah back to the nursery so I didn't fall asleep holding her. They wheeled her out and I dropped to much needed sleep, knowing the next day would be the hardest day of my life.

I was awoken the next morning by the cries of newborns down the hall. I quickly roused myself, excited to see Sarah again and to hold her. I rang the nurse button and requested Sarah to be brought in. Again, I waited much longer than necessary, long enough to feel that old impatience rising. She was even more beautiful after a night of rest. Her skin was pink and the softest I had ever touched. I fed her and watched, entranced, as she sucked on the bottle, cheeks and lips moving rhythmically. Every moment was important.

It wouldn't be long before I met James and Lisa. I imagined that they hadn't slept well, although I sure did. My young age worked in my favor, hastening my recovery. The nurse came back to ask if I wanted to get ready for the day. I agreed that I did and she let me know that, while Sarah would be discharged that day, I had to stay another night for observation. My face fell and the nurse immediately backpedaled. She assured me that Sarah could stay for another night, if I wanted. Of course I wanted! How could I stay there without Sarah? I mentally concluded that we would both leave the next day.

As sure as I felt, I still wasn't ready. I was probably less ready than when Sarah had still been inside of me. I took a deep, fortifying breath. Today was special; I was going to meet her parents. It's true, I was jealous of what they'd have, but I loved them anyway and they gave me hope for my daughter's future. I had faith that they were the best choice.

In the shower, I noticed my belly for the first time since I'd given birth. The hot water felt amazing on my achy body, but it was really strange to see how deflated I'd become. It had become less than half the size it was only 24 hours ago. As I prepared, my mom and dad stopped by to say good morning and let me know that they'd come back later. I blow-dried my hair and touched on a small amount of makeup. I wanted to make a good impression. I really wanted James and Lisa to like me. I didn't want to come off as some careless, ungodly teenager. Hopefully, they'd see deeper than the situation. The hospital said they'd let us use a meeting room. I sat, chewing my lip and tapping my foot. I resisted the urge to keep touching my hair, trying to look more presentable.

Finally, Brenda came in and asked if I was ready. I don't think I said anything in response. There was no way I could be ready! What did she expect me to say? Nevertheless, I followed her. At first, I wondered why we'd been given an entire meeting room, but my question was soon answered. My mom, dad, senior pastor, and his wife had all come. I was surprised to see the pastor, that he'd been willing to travel the over three-hour journey. Brenda had also brought an additional social worker named Olivia. There were still two empty seats. I stared at them, thinking about how those seats would hold Sarah's mother and father. It was honestly amazing. Those seats would hold the rest of her life. She'd never met them and neither had I. And, yet, those seats would be filled, just as surely as my baby's needs.

While we waited, Brenda and Olivia shared some words of wisdom about the mechanics of the adoption meeting. Instructions not to share personal information like my full name or the city I hailed from. To watch what I said. They said it was to prevent anything that might cause insecurity, but I just wanted to be myself. I didn't want to start off worried about conversational landmines. These people were sharing my most prized possession that I made inside my body. And they were telling me I couldn't share my own name? Really? That seemed absurd. They were getting my everything already and they couldn't have my name? My name was nothing in comparison, such a small detail in the face of my child. None of the adults understood when I laughed at how ridiculous that advice was; how could I expect them to? The minutes ticked by, the air thick with awkwardness and anxiety. They still saw this as an interview; only I knew that my mind was made up. For me, I was waiting for my daughter's parents to walk in. The decision had been made, with God's help. Who was I to disagree with His guidance? I was preparing to meet them and start building our lifelong relationship.

When they finally arrived, everyone looked up. I had seen their pictures, so I knew what to expect. In person, they were even more precious. So loving and excited! I did see some reservations, some insecurity on their faces, and I felt like it was my job to ease those fears. The youngest in the room, but I shouldered the responsibility with a smile. I had to let them know that this wasn't a "maybe" or a "let's get their hopes up, but I'm still deciding" kind of meeting. This was the first day of the rest of their lives.

As our eyes connected, I smiled widely. Under her breath, I heard Lisa mutter "Oh, thank God." I wondered what she meant. My eyes moved to James. He looked strong, but gentle, and I could see that he was the kind of man who would make a great father. Exactly what Sarah deserved. They sat down and I immediately queried:

"What did that mean? 'Oh, thank God'?"

"You know, they prepare us for everything in the adoption process. They said you could be so many things. We had no idea what you would look like or what to expect at all. And when I saw you, I was so happy. You're so lovely."

In that moment, I knew they saw me as I truly am. We spent the hours getting acquainted. Mostly it involved the adults talking to each other about me, about my baby. I felt left out at many points. For the first time, though, I began to comprehend that the dialogue over me was really just to protect Sarah and me. Anyway, I was busy trying to parse out a complicated tangle of emotions. Happiness, grief, excitement, and jealousy. I was excited to help these people who'd wanted a baby for so long finally achieve that joy. It was amazing to be able to give them their greatest wish. I've always cherished giving presents; it's one of the ways that I show love. I was able to change their lives, and that brought a sense of deep contentment.

I was also anxious for them to meet Sarah. After all, she was the reason everyone had gathered. I wanted to see their faces when they saw her. Her soft fair skin and rosy cheeks...I wanted to finish the formalities and move on to the main event! It wasn't that I wanted to rush, but I wanted us all to be with Sarah. I hated the thought of her being surrounded by strangers and other newborns when her family was right here, so close and yet, so far. Several times, I tried asking:

"Can we bring Sarah in? Let's bring Sarah in with us. I want you to meet Sarah."

Brenda kept brushing me off and reassuring me that we'd do it soon, we just needed to finish with the questions. I was more focused on us building our familial relationship and, for that, we needed Sarah. I wanted to see Lisa and James fall in love with her.

Finally, a nurse wheeled in the familiar clear, rectangular bed. At first, my gaze locked on to Sarah. I'd barely had any time with her since the hospital staff had interfered so much. Quickly, though, I turned to Lisa and James. I wanted to witness this moment and soak it all in. I had to see the moment they first met their daughter. Lisa's face softened and I knew what she saw. A baby girl, perfectly petite and with the cutest nose imaginable. The star of the show had arrived! The love in Lisa's eyes far outshone the fears and the hope was clear on her face. James put his arm around Lisa, though whether to comfort her or himself, I wasn't sure. I told them that they could hold Sarah.

I was so proud to have made such a perfect baby. First Lisa, then James, held her. Sarah was dwarfed by his strong arms, and she looked even tinier. I could see how careful and protective he was. I knew she'd be loved. I lost track of time during that meeting. Nobody had anywhere else they needed to be. That sterile meeting room in a hospital was the most important place that day. My parents took turns holding Sarah as well. There were many laughs and just as many tears. My eyes were swollen from crying so much. I felt like I was running out of time, that I had to explain how much I loved Sarah, and there weren't enough words or hours. I wanted Lisa and James to know me, to see me as family too. I'd never seen my father cry, but he did in that room. It was disconcerting. I wouldn't see him cry again for many years, until his own father passed away. I never wanted that day, with everyone holding Sarah, to end.

Fatigue slowly crept up on me. At some point, the pastor and his wife left and, before I knew it, the time had come for everyone else to leave too. Through my exhaustion, I wanted to share one more thing with my daughter's parents.

"I'm so excited about her name. I love the name Sarah. And I'm so glad she has a name now, because I hated hearing the staff just call her by my last name."

I didn't say that exactly. What I said was my last name. Brenda immediately nudged me, frowning and whispered an admonishment. I hadn't meant to say it, but, also, I didn't care. It felt like such a petty correction overall. What was the agency afraid of? That Lisa and James would track me down with that information and try to return Sarah? Like an unsatisfactory store-bought item? I would think they'd be more concerned about keeping their own last name private. Plenty of birth moms have changed their minds; there is a window of opportunity to do so for a reason. I could understand the agency or potential adoptive parents being wary of a birth mom who wanted to stalk them or take back their biological child, but the reverse scenario seemed too bizarre to imagine. I wouldn't hide. I was there, present, and myself. I told Brenda it didn't matter, but she scolded me anyway, telling me not to let it happen again. Which, frankly, seemed even weirder.

Overlooking the adoption faux pas, James and Lisa prepared to leave. They'd come back the next day to take Sarah home when I was discharged from the hospital. I would get to be alone with Sarah for one more night! Suddenly, my mouth opened, and I was as surprised as anyone to hear myself speak.

"Oh, you forgot something."

Lisa turned around with a polite smile, a question in her eyes.

"You can take her now."

Everyone's jaws collectively dropped. The social workers, the nurse, Lisa, and James. No one had expected her to be taken that night.

"Wait, are you sure?"

"She's medically cleared to be released. She should be with you."

It wasn't my intention to cause undue stress on everyone, but I probably did with that sudden announcement. Everyone began rushing around to get Sarah ready to leave. The nurses scattered to gather the paperwork, the social workers fumbled through their bags to get the contracts that still needed signing. I ended up signing so many papers that my hands cramped a few times. For me, and likely me alone, it was so simple. Sarah had been born. She was healthy. There was no need to spend another night apart from her parents. I wanted a few more moments with her, to finally say the one thing I hadn't so far. I knew I'd never be ready to let her go. But, I was going to do the right thing. Because I love her.

I had to say it now. I'd been avoiding it, trying to make each second with Sarah a happy, blessed one. But the time had finally come. I'd dreaded this moment for months, denied its eventuality, and done everything I could to not think about it. I had to say goodbye. I held Sarah, knowing it'd be the last time, at least for now. I couldn't stop thinking that she was more beautiful than anything in my wildest dreams. Tears I'd thought had finally dried up poured down my cheeks once more. She would not remember, but I would never forget.

"The past nine months we've been together have been the hardest, but most rewarding time of my life. I've never been embarrassed or ashamed of you. You have been my life and my happiness. If I didn't love you so very, very much, I'd keep you for myself. It'd be an honor to be your mom. But, I want you to have it all! A mom, a dad, maybe brothers and sisters, a stable environment, everything I can't give you now. I'm letting go of you for your own good, my sweet girl.

Today you met your new parents that God has sent us. They will love and protect you the way I wish I could. I've chosen them with care. I've done all that God has called me to do as your mother. This moment may be our last for now, so I'll say goodbye, but not farewell forever. I love you, my sweetie. My angel. Goodbye!"

Near hysterics, I desperately needed to rest. I had nothing left to give. My body crumpled to my bed, the anguish overwhelming. The grief was beyond my comprehension. She was gone. Sooner than expected, but I knew it was the right thing to do. Giving her up meant giving her unselfishly and without regret. When I was alone, everything ached. It was too much for me to handle, but I had no choice. I made it through the toughest day of my life. I couldn't contemplate tomorrow, the day after, or the rest of my life. I could only process that moment. I felt like I'd suffocate with how hard the grief gripped my lungs. At some point, I must have fallen asleep. I didn't get to sleep long, though, because I was soon woken by Brenda. Confusion washed over my tired mind. She told me that Lisa and James were about to leave and asked if I wanted to say one last goodbye.

A burst of excitement jolted me awake. She wasn't gone! Sarah was still here! I looked around and saw it was night. I was surprised they had stayed for so long. I dragged myself into the hall where they stood, proudly carrying Sarah in their arms. I asked Lisa for permission to hold her. She seemed surprised that I'd asked, but I'd signed away my right to hold Sarah. I wanted to respect everyone's new roles. Roles that they were only just stepping into. She said of course, and gently transferred Sarah into my arms. I no longer had any words; I'd said everything already. My heart reached out to that tiny little girl with all the love I could muster. I brushed my lips over her forehead in a gentle kiss. She smelled like a fresh new day. As I gave her back, my arms trembled slightly. It was really it this time.

Brenda came by my room later, to tell me that they had left. When she asked how I was, I simply replied "tired," and she agreed that I should rest. She told me what a great job I'd done and how proud of me she was. Apparently, Lisa and James had been very impressed with me and she was very happy for us. I couldn't participate in the conversation, just nodded and accepted her words. I was too drained. There was nothing more to say, do, or feel. My body's pain was at the forefront of my thoughts. I needed to sleep. Brenda had one more surprise for me, though.

"Since you didn't have the chance to meet with Lisa and James before, they've arranged for a meeting in six weeks. Is that okay?"

I couldn't believe what I heard. Sparks of joy lit up my exhausted mind. I would get to see Sarah again, and it would be soon! My heart skipped a beat and the very last of my energy soared through my veins. With that, I felt complete and I passed out soon after.

# EIGHT

# *Undefined by Anger*

*""Be angry, and do not sin": do not let the sun go down on your wrath..."*
*(Ephesians 4:26).*

Iawoke in the early hours of the morning, after only a few more hours of sleep. I laid in the bed, listening to the ringing silence of the hospital. Instinctually, I reached down to rub my stomach, but it was eerily flat. A deep loneliness seeped into my bones. I retreated into the wonderings I'd practiced when getting ready to let Sarah go. What was Sarah doing? Was she also awake? Is she in someone's arms or is she alone too? The questions were familiar ones, but the accompanying emotion was new. I tried to console my empty belly, but the rubbing only brought home the reality that she was gone. I wondered if it would ever get easier. Could I live this way long enough to find out? The answer terrified me. But, I firmly reminded myself that it was a fresh wound and, besides, I was tired. I needed rest. This was a journey that'd last my whole life; I'd only just embarked.

I managed to fall back asleep for a little while longer because the next thing I remember, a newborn's cry reached my ears.

The cry seemed to engage some maternal instinct I hadn't expected. My breasts suddenly hurt and were heavy in an unfamiliar way. Soon, I found myself laying in a puddle of warm milk. For some reason, it never occurred to me that I'd be in this situation. I sat up to get my bearings. Why didn't anyone warn me about this? I'd spoken to two social workers who specialized in adoption, Shelly, plenty of nurses, and even my own mother. Why hadn't any of those women, any of those adults warn me? I frowned and noticed that the crying hadn't let up. It was in the same room as me. Another mother had been brought in to share the room. I managed to say hi, somewhat taken aback by her presence. She smiled back at me in the barely lit room and asked where my baby was.

That was my first opportunity to be strong and to share my story with pride and confidence. I sat there, cold, wet, and remembered my commitment to having no regrets.

"Today was the happiest day of my life. I got to give my baby to her new mom and dad."

She looked at me, studying my face for any hint of a lie. I couldn't keep up the calm facade for very long, and I soon broke down crying. Her empathy was so strong that she couldn't help crying with me.

"If you're so happy, why are you crying?"

"I'm not happy, but it was the happiest day of my life. I gave my daughter a lifetime of stability."

We cried over my story. At one point, she allowed me to hold her baby. Without hesitation, I accepted. The baby began crying too, mimicking our tears. We all sobbed together. Those moments there, in a hospital with a total stranger, was one of the many that God would send my way to help me heal. I think she probably remembers that night too. The next day, I exited that quiet, liminal space and returned to my temporary home.

I expected to return to school too. No one had told me that I'd have to stay home for weeks in recovery. I thought that sounded mind-numbingly depressing and was eager to resume having something to occasionally take my mind off of Sarah. Shelly ended up explaining to me that I'd have to stay home for at least a couple of weeks in order to give my body a chance to fully rest, even though I was very young and healthy. She told me that most women allow six weeks, but I might be able to cut that time down if I felt strong enough. That wasn't all she had to tell me, though. She sat on the edge of my bed, clearly struggling with the words.

"Your mom and dad called. They want you to come home now."

I immediately protested. What about school? I was in the middle of the year! My grades would surely suffer if I left. I didn't want to be held back or have to repeat classes. I just wasn't prepared to go home yet. Leaving meant saying more goodbyes. A total separation from life with my daughter. The friends that I made who were undoubtedly curious about Sarah's birth and my well-being. Though I didn't know where Sarah lived, I suspected that it was in Los Angeles and leaving would also take me farther away from her. Shelly looked away, unable to keep holding my gaze.

"I'm sorry. Your parents are insisting. You don't have a choice."

I was so angry, so betrayed. I had done what they wanted! I gave my daughter up! I let myself be uprooted for reasons I didn't understand, be forced to live with a strange family and go to a strange school. I had moved here, chosen adoption, and now was going to be yanked back like some kind of puppet on a string? I was so sick and tired of having no choice in my life. Frustrated that no one in my life was willing to listen to me or respect my choices. I pleaded with my parents to let me stay at least until the end of the semester. My pleas fell on deaf ears. I couldn't believe that, after everything I'd done to demonstrate my own maturity and capability of making decisions, that my parents still would demean my autonomy so thoroughly. The end of the semester would have allowed me to finish my classes and there was a break anyway for Christmas. It would have been the perfect time to move home, but it was not to be.

After a few days of recovery, my mom came down to help move me back. I tried not to resent her too much, but the bitter anger still left a sour taste in my throat. She drove me to the high school, praying aloud that I would be allowed to transfer some of my credits to my old school and not have to repeat everything. When we arrived, we were greeted kindly. I'd become renowned at the school in my time there. I was immediately bombarded by questions regarding the lack of a baby bump and I fended them off with as much of a smile as I could muster. After a short discussion with the guidance counselor, we were informed that if each teacher was willing to sign off on my grade for the semester, I would be allowed to have those credits transferred. My mom was ecstatic, and I was happy that she was happy.

I felt bad for interrupting my first period class. My mom waited nearby, and I opened the door, already apologetic. Several students began shouting out congratulations and asking whether it had been a boy or girl. Their cheers warmed my heart, but they made me a little bittersweet too. I'd been accepted somewhere I'd been so sure I'd be completely out of place. To my surprise, my teacher greeted me with a smile and told me:

"I'm so proud of you. I cannot imagine what you're going through."

When I asked if she'd be willing to sign off on my grade, she had no qualms about giving me full credit. Mom and I rejoiced with the first success, the confidence bolstering our walk to the next teacher. One after another, I received the same result. My teachers had watched, for the past three months, as I dutifully arrived to class and gave my education my all, despite the challenges I faced, both mentally and physically. They honored my commitment by giving me full credit. My mother and I were thrilled. There was one more stop I wanted to make, practically bouncing with glee. I knew I couldn't leave without saying goodbye to a very special woman, someone I considered a friend and a mentor. I owed her sincere gratitude for everything she'd done. As we approached Nurse Patty's office, I saw the sign said Out to Lunch. My chest felt hot and the panic set in. No! I didn't want to leave without thanking her, but we must.

I never went back to that school. I never went back to the school nurse that I'd so thoroughly bonded with. My world spun out of control and everyone else controlled my every move. None of it was fair. I had no agency as a human being or as the adult I'd been forced to become. As we drove home, part of me did understand why my parents were being such control freaks. They were trying to protect me and do what they thought was right. I left their home, their child, and now I was coming home a mother, without her child. It hardly made sense, but I knew where they were coming from. It didn't mean I had to like it or agree with their choices.

In those initial weeks home, I was so lost. So alone. My seventeenth birthday came and went relatively uneventful. Only a sadness that Sarah had come too soon; that we should have shared a birthday. When night fell, I'd curl up for hours, imagining what Sarah might be doing, daydreaming about when I'd see her again. I wondered if she'd attend my wedding someday, maybe as a flower girl. Those hours of vivid imaginings robbed me of the rest my body craved. I was exhausted. I began setting up a space on the living room couch to sleep in and keep the TV on. At least with the background noise and images to distract me, there was a higher chance I'd fall asleep. I didn't know it then, but that habit would follow me for the rest of my life. That the dark of the night would forever represent a time of mind racing and lack of sleep. Night after night, I made my bed on the couch, trying to stop thinking about Sarah just long enough to drop off.

Two weeks after I'd returned, I received a letter in the mail. It was from Nurse Patty. I nervously opened the envelope, wondering what parting words of hope and wisdom she chose to impart. She'd always given me such wonderful support and the fact that she wrote really touched my heart. I missed her encouragement already. She wished me well and promised to always keep me in her prayers. I never heard from her again, but, deep down, I know she kept her promise. She was placed in my life during a time when I needed her the most, a guardian angel sent to watch over me.

In early January, I received what would be the first of many letters and pictures from Lisa and James. When I saw the envelope listing the adoption agency as the return address, I immediately tore it open, knowing what precious information would be inside. I could hardly wait to see the contents! There was a letter from Lisa, two and a half pages long. Her words were a balm, soothing the depressed loneliness I'd been wallowing in. I soaked in the words, the underlines, the hand-drawn hearts.

She talked about Sarah's first weeks at home, how she was able to meet a doting grandmother who fell in love with her tiny face at first

146

sight. Lisa wrote that she knew exactly why Sarah was such a peaceful and contented baby. It was because of me, my love for her and my love for Jesus. The fact that I nurtured her in my womb and prayed over her each day. Those words were a blessing, but the pictures even more so. I studied every detail in those photographs, trying to identify every toy in the background, the couch, the rug, the expressions on each person's face. I knew that I hadn't chosen these perfect parents; God had. I was simply His vessel to deliver Sarah into their arms.

I received a second letter prior to our visit which I treasured just as much as the first. Those letters brought me such joy and fulfillment. It gave me peace of mind, knowing that I'd definitely made the right decision. I wouldn't ever walk through a mall, wondering whether any girl I saw was mine, because I would know.

I was incredibly anxious for those six weeks to pass. I wanted to see Sarah again! The meeting was set for February, and it was all that I could think about. She would be six weeks old, how much would she have grown and changed? I'd get to see her, get to hold her, get to hear all that she had been doing...I started a countdown for the date. I marked each day on my calendar. When there were four weeks left, I made a paper link chain—28 links, one for each day. When I woke up, I'd tear off another link, indicating that I was one day closer to seeing Sarah again.

The day finally arrived. I stayed at my grandparents' house the night before. They lived in LA and I wanted to be as close as possible to ensure I wouldn't be late. I chose my clothes carefully, eager to keep up the good impression. Last time, they'd just seen me in a hospital gown, but, since then, I'd lost 25 pounds and could fit into my acid wash jeans again. I paired them with a burgundy shirt and inspected myself in a mirror. When I pronounced myself acceptable, I set out for the meeting. My grandfather warned me that the rainstorm was going to be bad, but I didn't know just how right he'd be. The rain crashed viciously into my windshield as I inched along the highway. I would certainly be late, but so would they. Nobody was going anywhere fast that day. I was in the biggest storm I'd ever seen! To this day, I've never seen such intense rain. At the time, I was determined to make it and nothing would stop me, especially not some rain.

I was really worried that something would happen that would prevent me from making it. I kept waiting for the other shoe to drop, for the rug to be yanked out from under me like it had so many times before. Luckily, nothing happened. I arrived before James and Lisa did, which gave me time to go to the bathroom and freshen up. It also gave me time to speak to Brenda. Brenda offered her usual small talk, but made sure I knew how to conduct myself. She explained how nervous Lisa and James were about the meeting. They were afraid I'd change my mind and take Sarah back. I knew that birth moms had a full year to change their minds, but it didn't seem fair to do that. I wondered why anyone would do such a thing. I assured Brenda that that was not the case. I was kind of surprised that Lisa and James would think I'd do that, but mostly it was disappointing. It showed that perhaps they really didn't know anything at all about me. I had thought they understood me better than that, that they considered me family as much as I considered them.

They arrived, somewhat frazzled by the weather, and Sarah was very clearly upset. Lisa looked to me nervously and I immediately reassured them that I had no plans to reclaim Sarah. I don't know whether they believed me; I didn't see any signs of relief on their faces. Instead, Lisa apologized for Sarah crying. She told me that Sarah was usually a very calm baby, and not so fussy. She insisted that Sarah was an easy baby and was already sleeping well at night. I didn't care about the crying. I wasn't sure why she apologized. I was just so happy to see them all again. Though she was still quite tiny, Sarah had grown a lot! Her hair was longer, with a little bit of curl and an auburn tone. She wore a pale pink outfit. Looking at them, it felt like they'd always been a part of my life and they always would be.

Lisa asked me if I wanted to hold Sarah, which was what I'd been hoping for the whole time. Really, for the whole six weeks we'd been apart. Sarah was still bawling when Lisa gently handed her to me. Initially, I drew her close to my chest, savoring the feeling of her body against mine, but then I held her out to get a good look at her. I stared into her beautiful blue eyes, tiny eyes still scrunched up in discomfort from the car ride. I softly spoke to her:

"Hi, Sarah."

The second I addressed her, she stopped crying. A single tear perched on her cheek as she stared attentively at me. Lisa blinked, taken aback and impressed by the reaction.

"Oh my goodness! She knows your voice!"

She knew my voice! That moment became etched in my mind, even now, thirty years later. Lisa took a picture of that moment and I cherish both the picture and those memories. It was a wonderful, cheerful visit. I felt such overwhelming joy. I couldn't wait to see them again. I didn't know when it would be, but I knew some time would have to pass. In the meantime, I looked forward to their letters and pictures. I was excited to move forward with my life. Moving forward, as opposed to moving on. I found it to be an important linguistic distinction. Many people, some with good intentions, told me that I had to move on. It was completely unrealistic. I was never going to "move on" without Sarah, but I could move forward. I took her with me for the rest of my life.

Moving forward would mean living a life that, one day, Sarah could look back on and be proud of. I would move forward by keeping her with me. She was my drive while I was pregnant and she'd continue to be my motivation in every major choice I'd make over the years.

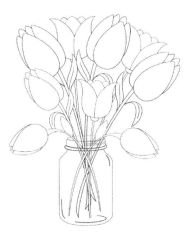

# NINE

## *Undefined by Fear*

*"My flesh and my heart fail; But God is the strength of my heart and my portion forever." (Psalms 73:26)*

The first year after Sarah's birth was filled with many changes. My parents had decided that it would be best for me to attend a different high school. They chose one clear across town. Yet another decision for me about which I wasn't consulted. They were hoping that I could avoid the judgement of my peers and have a fresh start there. I'd have put up more of a fight, but Kerri and Alia both transferred to this new school as well. I knew I'd have them at least. However, we didn't plan on the school going on strike for five weeks after my return home. That strike left me with far too much time on my hands. I began working out regularly. I would spend six to eight hours a day in the gym and ate minimally. I didn't understand at the time that I was simply seeking control in my life, battling a depression that had hit me hard. My parents dictated so much of my life, controlled my every move.

One day, my mother noticed how thin I'd become, even thinner than before I'd gotten pregnant. She insisted that I was no longer allowed to lose any more weight. Screams of outrage echoed in my head. I can't lose weight? That was my breaking point. She couldn't dictate what I did or did not eat. At seventeen, I had money, a car, and access to my food, whether or not I chose to eat it. The intense depression I experienced that year terrified me. I could hardly remember the outgoing, playful teen I'd once been. I had lost my ambition, my motivation, and any connection to the people who loved me. Sending me away for months during such a vulnerable time with minimal contact had managed to sever those relationships in ways I couldn't yet comprehend. Something had to change; I couldn't go on like this.

I was working out at the gym, like most days, when suddenly, I passed out. My body could no longer withstand the punishing treatment. I allowed myself a single taco each day and exercised many hours. My usual weight of 130 was down to 118 lbs. I examined it every day in the mirror; it wasn't skeletal or even necessarily worrying, but it was much smaller than I naturally maintained. Passing out scared me, and I knew I couldn't keep living this way. I scarcely recognized myself.

Fortunately, school started back up soon after I'd made that decision, and I was able to steer my focus onto that instead. I thought life would go back to normal, but I underestimated the depths of my own depression. My only saving grace that year was that, almost every month, I would receive new letters and pictures from Lisa and James. I considered those letters my lifeline. It was the only thing I'd look forward to. No sooner would one arrive than I'd start counting down the days until I'd get another. Sarah grew, acquiring teeth, getting more hair, and I kept an obsessive chronicle of her life. She was so adorable, so happy! I memorized the details of every picture. I wanted to see the wallpaper in the background, the pillows on the couches, the curtains, the carpet, what everyone was wearing. I needed to be able to accurately visualize Sarah and her home. I studied the photographs with care, smiling as I remembered counting her fingers and toes in the hospital.

They were the only thing that helped me heal that first year. When they told me that Sarah had her first cold, I imagined her little nose running. How they must have had to wipe that adorable nose so many times. I saw it all play out in the confines of my mind. The words on paper became real to me. I let my imagination fill in the blanks and replayed scenes over and over in vivid daydreams. Lisa and James discussed their church, their lives, and their everyday activities. I pictured the drive to church: They'd put Sarah in the car seat and neatly tuck her in. She'd be dressed in pink, clean, fresh, and beautiful. I soaked it all in. It gave me renewed life, those reminders of peace and contentment in my decision and why I kept living. I checked the mail daily for new letters, it became my new way of life.

After the first year came to an end, I received a call from Brenda. She wanted to know how I was coping. I came clean about my depression and explained that I needed counseling. I asked if there were any options through the agency. She said there were, but she dismissed the option, saying I lived too far away to make use of it. She didn't give me any advice about seeking out alternative methods or even address what I'd just told her; she'd called with a different purpose. She wanted me to know that, now that the first year had passed, James and Lisa would be transitioning to only a single letter a year. Once a year? I was totally taken aback! Brenda assured me that it was standard procedure, and I shouldn't take it personally. That I hadn't done anything wrong. I was relieved to hear that, but bewildered because no one had explained that to me. Why was I only hearing about this now? I tried to console myself by asking Brenda when they would be ready for another visit since it had been almost a year.

She brushed away my request, as if it was something casual. She gave me some excuse about giving them more time to bond with Sarah before we discussed meeting any further. Although I didn't like Brenda's responses, and honestly felt that the agency had deceived and cheated me over and over again, I respected that Lisa and James must need a little more time. I still trusted Brenda to be an expert and to know what everyone needed. Little did I know, she was only looking out for the agency's interests, not mine, not James and Lisa's, and certainly not Sarah's. I can only hope that things have changed in the intervening years.

For the following six months, I continued to spiral. I began dating again to regain control in one of the only ways available to me, and remained immersed in a deep, undiagnosed depression. Because of that, I made many unhealthy choices, ones I wasn't proud of. In my heart, I still loved God and my family. I still had strong moral and spiritual beliefs. I even knew that my parents' controlling behavior was to help guide and protect me for an outcome that would be best. But, that knowledge was buried deeply, and, back then, out of reach. In the midst of everything, I tried to fight through. I wanted to be the best version of myself. I wanted to live a life that both Sarah and I could be proud of. The struggle was too difficult to overcome. I was hopeless, listless, and without interest in any of the things I used to love. I slept too much and couldn't control my emotions.

Things reached a head one night, after I'd set up my bed on the couch. I stepped away briefly to brush my teeth and didn't see my brother sneak in and hide under the couch cushion to scare me. It was typical, obnoxious, and ultimately harmless little brother behavior. I laid down to settle in, completely unawares. He playfully roared and moved the cushions I'd just laid on. I screamed, immediately frantic. It didn't matter that he came out right away, prepared for it to all be a big joke. I tipped into hysterics, totally inconsolable. I regret how much our father scolded him for the prank. I knew he didn't mean any harm, but I couldn't stop my overreaction.

That loss of control permeated my life. Despite my desire to live a life my daughter could be proud of, decision after decision, I became more impulsive and continued not to reflect that desire. My careless behavior led me to be pregnant again, only fifteen months after I'd given birth to Sarah. That time, there was no one to blame but myself. My own choices had led to it; I hadn't been forced or coerced.

My parents found out and insisted that I choose adoption once more. Lisa and James would likely welcome a sibling for Sarah. Although the thought of Sarah becoming a big sister brought me a smile, I knew what I had to do. I had to pull myself up and get back on track, to rededicate my life to serving God and ask for His forgiveness. Maybe even forgive myself. It wouldn't be easy, but it was necessary, and this was the wake-up call I needed. I refused to waste away grieving. I prayed to be healed from the hurt and the pain that plagued my every waking moment. That God would, once again, save me, as He had so many times before. I would have to make important decisions; it was time to grow up, once and for all. This time, I'd be the one making the choices.

To become a mom to my son, I'd have to leave the anger and the juvenile behavior behind. I surrendered to God and to my own commitment of living a life determined for success. Faced with another pregnancy, still a teenager, now in my senior year, it once again brought me maturity far beyond my years. It gave me back my motivation to do the right thing. I'd be a single mom, not my ideal, but I wouldn't give up another child. I knew I could take care of my son and be the mother he deserved. This time, I'd be going against my parents' wishes. Standing up for myself was terrifying; it wouldn't be easy, nor well-received in my household. I finally found my voice.

Fortunately, my parents' love for me far outweighed their disappointment. They would learn to accept and embrace my decision. A few months into the second pregnancy, I received an unexpected call from Brenda. I'd come to dread hearing from her; she never wanted to give me good news. Without much explanation, or small-talk I'd come to expect from her, she launched into a series of questions. Her tone was serious and anxiety crept down my spine. Questions like:

"Does anyone in your family suffer from malnutrition? Does anyone in your family suffer from anemia?"

I didn't understand the relevance, but I quickly assured her that no one did. I reminded her that I have asthma, but she would have known that from having access to my health records. I told her to wait while I double-checked my information with my mom. Mom confirmed that no one in our family had those kinds of medical issues. I reaffirmed that information to Brenda. She told me that she would keep me posted, but that she was calling on behalf of James and Lisa who were having concerns about Sarah's health. I begged her to tell me more, at least to tell me if Sarah was okay. Brenda refused to share any further information. I waited nervously for a few weeks to hear back about my daughter. Was it some kind of illness? A disease? Was it inherited from me or caught from her environment? If it was genetic, would the son I was pregnant with now also have it? None of my increasingly frantic questions prepared me for the news.

Brenda finally called back and told me that Sarah had been diagnosed with a genetic disease called Cystic Fibrosis. That the disease was terminal and her life expectancy only went through childhood. I was devastated. I knew what cystic fibrosis was, though no one in my family had ever had it. It is a progressively degenerative disease; one that causes lung infections and makes it difficult to breathe. I knew, too, that it is always fatal. One of my childhood friends had it, and he'd passed away at nine years old. I remembered, vividly, how he'd told me that he was going to "Teddy Bear Heaven" only months before he passed. My heart sank. How did she end up with it? Was it my fault? Did I do something wrong? Thousands of questions ran through my head, but none of them emerged.

"Did you hear me?"

My throat constricted; I couldn't speak.

"I know this is hard to hear, but imagine how hard it is for Lisa and James."

My heart went out to them. I couldn't process the anguish they had to be feeling. I remained silent, trying to understand everything that was happening. Brenda filled the empty space with words, intensely hurtful words that she could never take back. She ought to be ashamed of the way she continually mistreated a young mother, one who'd been through so much already.

"They didn't sign up for this, you know. They would never have taken her if they'd known Sarah was sick!"

I had no response. My heart clenched, I felt like I was suffocating. I wanted to scream "Then give her back! I'll take her back!" Even my thoughts went quiet in the face of either her excruciating cruelty or her gargantuan stupidity. Whether it was true or not, I don't know. It hardly mattered. I gave them a perfect baby, my baby, whom I knew they loved. Of course they wouldn't have chosen this for her, who would? Either way, there was no need for Brenda to say that. Many years later, I was able to recognize the supreme immaturity of the social worker, the panic she likely also felt, the questions about whether she'd done her job right. Wondering if she'd missed something in my medical background, something that could have led to this conclusion earlier. She wouldn't have found anything; my family had no idea we carried the gene.

My prayers went to Sarah. I tried not to imagine what kind of discomfort her tiny body might be in. How difficult it was as an eighteen-month-old struggling for breath. My heart ached for Lisa and James, the sleepless nights they would suffer, the impending fear. It didn't help that I had personally seen how cystic fibrosis took its toll on a child's body, to the point that they often wouldn't live to see double digits. There had been progress in the medical field and children were living longer, the prognosis was not good.

With all of that in mind, I experienced an even greater loss. The likelihood that this child, my daughter who I'd given up—with the intention to eventually reunite with—might not survive long enough for any of that to happen. I had hoped to share in her childhood and to befriend her as an adult, to share a special and unique bond. The words "terminal illness" dashed those hopes that had kept me going. Finding out that Sarah had cystic fibrosis changed me. It changed all of my plans for the future, knowing that they could be stripped away. If she didn't have an adulthood, how could I ever hope to find peace? How was I supposed to be okay? I knew I couldn't, not with that kind of thinking. I had to search for the strength within myself, to pray for her health and her life. I had to let go of my own selfish desires, my dreams for an adulthood relationship.

Adoption was not a one-time choice. It would have to be a decision I made, over and over again, as the layers of life unfolded. I realized that letting go is bigger than saying goodbye; it's bigger than hoping for tomorrow; it's choosing to be unselfish, no matter what the cost. A complete sacrifice of self, dreams, and desires. It would be total trust in God and His plans. It didn't happen overnight, but, over time, I began to work past the initial shock and disbelief, to move past the heartbreak I felt for Sarah and her family. The grief that far exceeded anything I'd ever known.

When I gave Sarah into James and Lisa's care, I hadn't fully released her. I'd let go with a hope of a lifetime together, the expectation that we'd reunite. I had not fully given her over into their hands or God's hands. I got stronger and reminded myself that God had created Sarah. He made her in my womb for James and Lisa. He made her to have a life, whatever life that might be. I thought again about the night in Montana, laying on the cold tile floor in a stranger's house when I was convinced I was having a miscarriage. I'd never forgotten God's promise to me that my baby would not die. Those words were true then and I still believe them today.

I held on to my new mantra: God is in control of Sarah's health. He is in control of her life. I used it to change my mindset, knowing that whatever the future holds, God is in control. That day, in my heart, I gave Sarah up. But not into the arms of James and Lisa, despite my trust in their good sense and love for my baby. Instead, I gave Sarah into His care, this time for good.

I finally decided that it was time to come clean to my parents about how Sarah had been conceived. I explained to them that I had been raped, my hands twisting together in anxiety and I haltingly revealed the circumstances. My parents were both shaken by the conversation, although my mom confessed that she had suspected, but hadn't wanted to force me to confront it if I wasn't ready. My father commented that it was probably a good thing that he hadn't known at the time because he worried what he might have done. He was a painfully shy man of few words, but he was super loving. His declaration meant a lot to me.

I continued to write to Lisa and James regularly. I still received my annual letter and pictures. Although they shared minimal information about Sarah's health, just enough to reassure me, it was never the primary message. Lisa often expressed her love and appreciation for me. She noted that Sarah had my smile. We were both taken aback by how much Daniel and Sarah resembled each other, their pale skin and freckles especially similar. Each time I wrote, I requested again a chance to meet face to face. I imagined the kids playing together, finally meeting one another. I often shared Sarah's pictures and spoke fondly of my extended family. However, a visit was never permitted.

I couldn't have known it then, but they never had any intention of having an open adoption. They had always requested that it be closed. The agency had lied to me, assuring me that James and Lisa had agreed to an open adoption, then promptly turned around and lied to them about my intentions. Each of my requests must have caused substantial confusion to them. Did they call the agency, asking why I wanted to meet? I wonder how the agency covered up their lies. Did they wonder whether it was due to Sarah's health? My hopes of a childhood reunion with my baby were never the plan. Years later, it saddens me to think about the pressure those requests likely caused, the bewilderment of having continuous rebuttals to their expectations.

At the time, I was intensely disappointed that every request was met with rejection—hurt that they had no desire to meet me and my beautiful, growing family. However, I respected their choice. As disappointed as I was, I knew they were looking out for Sarah's best interests. They were her parents, and I respected that. I had to let go not just of my baby, but also my own expectations. A childhood reunion was not to be. They wanted to keep Sarah just for themselves. I understood their perspective, especially now that her life was so uncertain. In no way did their decision diminish my love for them. I just kept moving forward. I made peace with the fact that I'd get my letter, once a year, and that would be that.

I spent my time working on myself as a person. It was vital that Sarah could one day see me for who I truly am. Not just a birth mom, or someone who'd made mistakes, but a good person. A person who was spirited, ambitious, outgoing, and loving. A woman who loves her, loves God, and loves her family. Someone Sarah could be proud of.

I went on to beat the odds of teenage parenting and obtained my associates degree, followed by a bachelor's, and finally a master's. Each step I took was a step closer to being the woman I wanted Sarah to see. Someone she'd be honored to call her birth mom. I prided myself in my parenting, embracing my subsequent children wholeheartedly. I could appreciate them so much, knowing how hard it'd been to give up Sarah.

One day, I received a phone call. It was the secretary from my old church. It was nice to hear from her; we'd always gotten along well. However, the small talk quickly faded as she informed me that she was calling about a very serious matter: There had been allegations of sexual misconduct that implicated a youth leader. The second she said that, I knew who she meant. I didn't need a name. My stomach instantly twisted into knots; what was she going to ask? More importantly, had he hurt someone else? Guilt stung as I realized that, by keeping mum about my experience, I'd left him free to assault more young girls.

The secretary haltingly explained that she was calling because I'd known the whole youth group so well. She wanted to know if anyone had confessed something along those lines to me, or if I had any information. In fact, someone had come forward, but I hadn't wanted to disclose the confessor's secret without permission. Instead, I shared my own story of assault. I did admit that I knew of another, but withheld her name. It was the first time I'd admitted what the youth leader had done. Years had passed; I'd moved on. I was an adult at that point, about to be married. I'd spent those years ignoring the magnitude of the pain he'd caused me, both physically and mentally. My opinion of authority was still tainted from the experience. The secretary told me she'd call back, but she had other calls to make.

A few days later, she did call again. This time, she had a plan. The youth leader had requested an opportunity to formally apologize to me.

"This would be done at the church, in the presence of two associate pastors, the youth leader, your parents, me, and, of course, you."

I held the phone away from my ear for a second, examining it in horror. Did she just say my parents? What was the church playing at? Why did they need to be involved? I couldn't fathom their reasoning or their ludicrous plan. I'd never told my parents about the second rape. I had put them through so much during those years; we were finally past all of that now! My life was on track, my wedding weeks away. Why would I throw all of that away just to make my rapist happy? To make the church happy? I argued with her.

"No way! This can't happen! I haven't told anyone about this except for you. I only told you to protect other young girls, not to go public. Why does he get to call a meeting? What if I refuse?"

She murmured her understanding and sympathies, but they rang hollow when she responded. Her words made chills run up and down my spine.

"We will be having the meeting, with or without you. We prefer that you come, but, of course, you do not have to. You should know, your parents have already agreed to come—"

I interrupted her.

"Did you tell them? Do they know what happened?"

"No, we just let them know that they should be present and they agreed."

Her tone remained calm. I asked if she knew of any other girls who the youth leader had assaulted, and she confirmed that she did. I wanted to know if they would be attending the meeting, or their parents, but she said

165

they would not. I couldn't believe that, after all these years, I would have to face this jerk! Once again, I had no control over the situation. Whether I went or not, they'd still be talking about me, discussing a very personal incident. Forget that! I managed not to vent my anger at the secretary, but I knew how I could take some control back. I wouldn't go. That was the plan, I just wouldn't go.

The morning of the meeting, I felt nauseated. My parents would have to sit there and hear about a tragic violation of their daughter, both spiritually and physically. They would be hurt, confused, and likely full of questions. Questions that I did not want to either hear nor answer. In an effort to avoid thinking about it, I went to breakfast with my fiancé. We met up when I knew the meeting would be held. Our coffee had arrived and we were waiting for our meal, but I couldn't get the toxic thoughts out of my head. I knew I should tell my fiancé; we were going to commit to sharing our lives together, after all. I didn't want to go into it much, though my appetite was already ruined, but I said it fast, like pulling off a Band-Aid.

"When I was pregnant with Sarah, I told my youth leader about it, and he raped me too. Now, today, the church is having a meeting because he wants to apologize. Also, the meeting starts now!"

It all came rushing out of me in one breath. There! I said it! When I finally looked up and made eye contact, he stared at me.

"Then why are we sitting here?"

He insisted that we should go. I argued that I didn't want to, I didn't have to go listen to my rapist excuse himself—like it was something he could say a cheap apology for and be over it.

"How can you be sure he'll tell the truth?"

Huh? I hadn't even thought about that. Why would he lie? Why call an apology meeting just to lie? That seemed counterproductive and it wouldn't do anything for his soul. God knew what happened and if he wanted forgiveness he should confess, but my heart sank as I realized that he really could say anything without me there. Maybe he'd even been counting on my absence. I should be there.

"We have to go!"

Without waiting around to explain to the waitress, we left enough cash on the table for our coffees and rushed out the door. When we arrived at the church, I could see that the meeting had just begun. I stormed into the room, somewhat out of breath from the adrenaline and frustration that now consumed me. This was one more indignity that he inflicted on me. My parents glanced up, surprised to see me. They still had no idea what the meeting was about. I wasn't too late! Loudly, I stated:

"The meeting can start now!"

The youth leader greeted me kindly and my skin crawled at his tone. He told me to have a seat.

"You don't get to tell me what to do."

I sneered at him and stood behind my chair. Everyone else shifted uncomfortably in their chairs. I was a little taken aback by the number of people in the room. The associate pastor opened the meeting with a prayer. I furiously kept my mouth shut and refused to join. I stewed in my fury, clenching and unclenching my fists. After the prayer, he briefly explained that we'd all been asked here today to hear the formal apology of the youth leader. He wanted to come clean about his sin and ask for forgiveness. Everyone knew what was meant, except for my parents, who were, by then, completely bemused. The associate pastor turned the floor over to the youth leader. I cringed at his voice: disgustingly calm, slyly spinning his evil.

"Thank you all for coming today. This is very hard for me."

I scoffed loudly. People rebuked me with their eyes, somehow expecting me to peacefully allow him to speak.

"I want to apologize for Michelle and my indiscretion. We got caught up in a moment of passion and I should not have let it happen."

What? What! What was he talking about? My brain whirred and my eyes widened. Lies! All lies! He explained how I'd come to him, in confidence, about being raped and I'd been looking for intimacy with him. He shouldn't have allowed it to go that far, but he did, and, for that, he was sorry. I stared at him in disbelief. Really? He actually thought that people would believe this crap?

"Liar."

"Excuse me?"

"I said: you're a liar."

I wasn't the passive, terrified little girl he remembered anymore. This time, I'd be assertive.

"If you were really sorry, you'd actually take responsibility. We both know that I'm not the only teenage girl you raped."

168

His eyes narrowed speculatively. Apparently, he hadn't known that I was aware of the others. I took the opportunity to continue.

"How dare you bring all of us here for your fake apology? And then lie about the circumstances? You put this burden on me and my parents. There was no way I would have willingly had sex with you. You're twice my age! I was a young girl, a child, reaching out to what should have been a safe haven. You violated my trust! Now, today, you continue to take from me what isn't yours."

He spluttered, caught off guard. He hadn't expected me to stand up to him, but I wasn't about to stand there and take it a second time. It was hardly a productive meeting for anybody. My parents were, understandably, shocked by his words and my unexpected replies. I held my head high and walked away from it confident that the people who mattered knew the truth. I clarified to my parents later, but they didn't need to discuss it; they knew I was telling the truth and were heartbroken and angry. That was fine; I didn't want to discuss it either. I forcibly put it out of my mind and focused on the important things in my life: my family.

When Sarah turned five, I received my annual letter. As always, I was happy for the update. Sarah was in good health and she'd had a great year. They shared how Sarah had accepted Jesus into her heart, which gave me real joy. I was so warmed that my daughter loved God as much as I did. The pictures were the biggest blessing; watching my beautiful daughter grow. A couple of days later, I got another letter with the adoption agency's familiar return address. Each letter was always sent via the agency so that we wouldn't know each other's addresses. We made sure not to share specifics; I didn't even know their last name. Anxious to know what had been sent, I opened the envelope immediately. It was nearly empty, but for a check inside.

For a moment, I wasn't sure what I was looking at. It was a personal check from Lisa and James to the adoption agency. It was a small amount, only five dollars, and marked as a donation. My hands shook as I processed the information. I couldn't stop looking at it, all of the information it contained about my daughter's family. I finally knew Sarah's last name. I knew her home address and phone number. How could this have happened? This must be some kind of weird mistake. It had obviously not been intended for me. This could cost someone their job. Hadn't Brenda warned me about this kind of situation? I keenly remembered the scolding I suffered at the hospital when I accidentally revealed my surname. The agency was lucky this had happened to me and not a birth mom who'd abuse the information.

Knowing Sarah's last name, though, brought healing I didn't even know I'd needed. It gave me some small measure of control. For so many years, people had taken away my control, over and over again, and now I had a little bit back. If I wanted to, I could show up at their front door. I could call and ask to speak to Sarah. I wouldn't, but it was powerful knowing that I could.

I knew I wasn't supposed to have that check. I called Brenda right away, telling her that somehow, a mistake had been made and I'd wound up with a check from James and Lisa for the agency. I assured her that everything would be okay; I didn't want her worrying that I would do something creepy or do anything that would harm Sarah.

"Let me stop you there," Brenda interjected.

"Yeah?"

"I already know what you're going to tell me."

"Wait—you know I got a check?"

"Well, let me put it this way. Of course I wouldn't know that. But, why don't you do this? Go ahead and mail it back. We'll get that deposited and no one will ever know that it came to you and you can just tuck that information away for the future. If you ever need it, you have it."

"Uh...I mean it's just crazy that this happened, right? If I were any other birth mom, this might be a real problem for the adoptive family and could bring legal problems to your agency. This is bad! If you had a crazy birth mom, this would be terrible."

"But you're not like that. We know that. I think that everything's just fine."

I could tell from the conversation that the check had been mailed to me on purpose. There was no other reasonable explanation. I couldn't figure out why they'd do it, though.

"Did you mean to send this to me? Was this on purpose?"

"Of course it's not!"

Brenda immediately protested, but with enough sarcasm in her voice that I didn't take her seriously.

"Michelle, you need to know that James and Lisa have gotten more insecure. At this point, they could be a flight risk."

A flight risk? What did that mean? That they would move away without telling anyone? That they were planning to leave the country? It was devastating enough that they didn't want to visit with me, but what would a flight risk mean? I didn't understand and I told Brenda so.

"We want to look out for you."

She insisted again that the check hadn't been sent on purpose and reassured me that she didn't believe I'd do anything harmful with that information. She let me know that multiple employees at the agency were concerned that James and Lisa were not in a good place currently. Brenda even apologized for the failure to go through with the open adoption as I'd requested. I didn't know that the agency was simply playing mind games at this point. They'd created doubts about me to Lisa and James around that time as well, trying to rile us both up and set us against each other. To this day, I don't know why they manipulated us like that. When I hung up, I felt a surge of guilt. What did I do? How could I fix this? Why are they feeling insecure? Did I say something wrong? Did they think I was trying to get Sarah back?

I wanted to be able to personally reassure them. Then I thought about Sarah's health. Maybe she was so sick that it was affecting them in other ways. Being in the dark was excruciating for me. I finally did as I'd been asked: photocopying the check and mailing the original back to the adoption agency. I would never know for sure why it had happened or whether it actually had been an accident.

It was around this time that I realized that I desperately wanted to have another daughter, one who I could raise myself. I was thankful when Daniel turned out to be a boy, so quickly after Sarah. I never wanted it to feel as though another child could replace her. Now married, I was also happy for a second son when Jacob arrived; I knew he'd be a wonderful friend and playmate with Daniel. I wanted a little girl. I was ecstatic to find out that I was pregnant again and hoped that my prayers for a girl would be answered.

172

Only a few months in, I felt my water break and had some bleeding. I visited the emergency room and saw multiple specialists. I was eternally grateful to learn that I was still pregnant. I'd been terrified that the bleeding indicated a miscarriage. To my surprise, they informed me that I had been carrying twins; the bleeding had been a miscarriage after all, but only one child had been lost. The doctors put me on bed rest after that. I was only in the first trimester, so it went on for six months. My faith was challenged during those months as I experienced intermittent contractions and bleeding during that time.

I had many ultrasounds, to see how my remaining child was doing. At one of them, the doctor explained that I'd need to come into the office and discuss my options. My heart raced as I put my clothes back on. What would he say? Now, five months in, I'd been feeling more confident that my baby would be healthy and survive to term. My stomach sank at his expression though; I sensed it would be bad news. I didn't have to wait for long.

I learned that there were several concerns for the life of my child. They'd identified a large cyst on the brain, covering nearly a fourth of the head. Apparently, it was forcing the head into a deformed shape, like a lemon. He gently broke the news that my baby might never be able to walk, talk, or go through a child's typical development. I was shocked to hear that there were missing vital organs as well. On top of everything else, some of the twin's tissue remained in my uterus and that decaying tissue was being absorbed into the healthy baby's amniotic sac and mixing, like floating confetti, in the amniotic fluid. These tissues would move in and out of the lungs as the baby practiced breathing with the amniotic fluid. The doctor anticipated that the tiny lungs could collapse after birth with the first attempts to breathe air. The reports were grave. He offered me some options, none of which would result in my baby coming home.

Although on bedrest, some days, I managed to get to church. My church fervently prayed for a miracle. On one of those days, I was approached by a godly man. He told me that God had shown him that my daughter would dance and sing, contrary to medical opinions. I held onto that hope with my whole heart. It kept me strong. The pregnancy continued and, in the last few weeks, I went in for another ultrasound. I prepared myself for the doctor's negative reaction, mentally squaring my shoulders. This time, we saw a miracle.

Each ultrasound began the same way: on the monitor, I'd see the empty sac, where my son or daughter had once grown, then we'd pan over to my child still inside. First, the nurse measured the head and cyst, but, this time, they couldn't see the cyst on the screen. The head had reformed into a normal shape and there was no evidence of any other growth. The doctor wasn't sure what he was seeing. He grabbed my file and reviewed the history, glancing back and forth between the paper and the screen. Every organ was accounted for, including the fingers and toes. I heard him murmur, under his breath, that it was truly remarkable.

"What's going on?"

He remained deep in thought and didn't respond. I began to shift nervously, until he finally faced me again.

"This is what we, in the medical field, call 'unexplainable!'"

I asked for more details, laying there anxiously.

"This baby is perfect and it is a girl. A perfectly healthy baby girl!"

Sheer relief overwhelmed me. I burst into tears. The weight of the past months had truly taken its toll on me. Could it be true? Was my baby really okay? It was the miracle I had been praying for.

I hadn't been expecting twins, so when I lost one, I didn't grieve much. I was too focused on my remaining child. However, when Rachel was two weeks old, my husband and I sat, watching TV, with Rachel laying on his legs. We were admiring her, commenting on how cute she was and what a blessing everything had been. Suddenly, my grief hit me. I saw my empty lap next to his and recognized that there should have been another child there too. Guilt flooded my heart; I hadn't even mourned for the child I'd lost. Together, my husband and I cried over our loss. I knew I'd never hide the fact that Rachel was a twin. I'd acknowledge her twin's life, just how I acknowledged Sarah's, though neither could be in my life.

The following year, with my annual letter, I received a photograph of Sarah on a trip to Disneyland. As always studying each angle of her face, and detail in the picture. That same year, my aunt Jennifer surprised the kids and I with our own trip to Disneyland, a luxury that I could not have afforded on my own. As we were rushing around the park hopping from ride to ride, I suddenly recognized the backdrop. I found the railing that James, Lisa and Sarah had posed on. I stopped dead in my tracks, with the reality sending a surge of adrenaline, but my actions slowing to almost a halt. I reached my hand to the very spot Sarah had sat. Her little body had been protected with mom and dad on both sides as she sat on top of the railing. I ran my hands over it gently and soaked in the moment.

Lisa and James, helped again through adoption, also welcomed another daughter, Rose, into their lives. A little sister for Sarah. I had always hoped she'd have siblings and now, at age seven, I knew she'd be thrilled to finally be a big sister. On Sarah's eighth birthday, I received my usual card and pictures. I saw the enlarged family standing around the Christmas tree, all smiles. It brought me great joy. The letter itself was quite insightful. I learned that Sarah was transitioning to being homeschooled, and she had been given an airway clearance system, a medical vest that normally cost $20,000! Lisa and James had been blessed and received the vest for free. I was relieved to know that Sarah was getting the medical help she needed and I imagined that her parents were equally relieved that they were getting the necessary resources to support her.

Though I cherished all of their letters, there was no indication that it was the last letter I'd ever receive from them and the next decade would be filled only with deafening silence. That I would be tested beyond anything I could have possibly imagined. I didn't know I'd have to let Sarah go again, to sever ties completely.

# TEN

# *Undefined by the Unknown*

*"Fear not, for I am with you; Be not dismayed, for I am your God. I will strengthen you, Yes, I will help you, I will uphold you with My righteous right hand." Isaiah 41:10*

When the following year found me with no letter from Lisa and James, I wondered if everything was okay. I didn't rush to judgement; maybe the letter was simply late or they were busy with something. I knew my own life was hectic with three little ones to take care of. Another month went by and I still received nothing. Then another. I began sharing the situation with some of my friends and family, asking for their input.

"I don't know what's going on. I haven't heard anything."

"What do you think is happening?"

My mom always cut straight to the point.

"Perhaps Sarah's health has taken a turn for the worse?" I'd hope that if she was critically ill or had passed away that at least the adoption agency would tell me, but with their track record...I didn't know.

She reassured me that the agency would definitely let me know if it was anything that serious. I wasn't convinced.

"Why don't you just call the agency if you're worried? Ask them. Tell them you haven't received your annual letter. It might have been lost in the mail."

"I don't want to be pushy about it. I don't want to call and ask for a letter. I'll give it more time; maybe Lisa and James took the girls on vacation and have been busy."

So, I waited. I waited an entire year. I realized that it was December again and hoped that, this year, I'd get my letter. Maybe last year had been a mistake and they'd been overwhelmed and forgotten. I gave it a couple of months again, knowing what a busy season Christmas could be with children. By February, I decided to call the adoption agency. The phone rang twice; I almost hung up. Part of me didn't want to know, to lose that hope I held onto for those letters. A girl I didn't recognize answered and I asked to speak with Brenda. A brief hold and then I heard her familiar voice on the line. After a quick reintroduction, it had been a few years after all, I explained the situation.

"I've got to check in on Sarah. I haven't heard an update in more than two years! I haven't received any letters and it's really unusual. They were really good about sending the letters and pictures so I just want to make sure that they're okay. Is Sarah okay? What's going on? Did her disease get worse? Did something happen to her?"

She quickly assured me that Sarah was alive and as well as could be expected with cystic fibrosis. Praise God! I felt my anxiety melt away until Brenda's next words penetrated my ears.

"Michelle. James and Lisa have now initiated the eight-year contract that you all signed and they're no longer planning to have contact with you, moving forward."

Her words felt like knives slicing at my soul. The wounds would take years to fully heal. I gasped and wasn't able to speak for some time. After a long silence, I asked:

"Wha— what are you talking about? What eight-year contract? I—I don't know what you're talking about! No one told me that!"

I never would have agreed to anything like that! I'd already been disappointed that the adoption hadn't been as open as I'd requested, as the agency had promised me it would be. This was beyond anything I could fathom. No contact? No one would even tell me, year to year, whether my daughter still lived? I'd have to call this stupid, lying agency if I wanted to know if my baby was still alive? What guarantee did I even have that Brenda wasn't lying now too?

"No, you signed it. This was part of the adoption agreement. Would you like us to fax over a copy of what you signed?"

"I have no doubt that you could fax me a copy of this ridiculous contract that you forced me to sign, but you never told me that I was signing an eight-year contract. You were responsible for me! That was never an expectation; you never even hinted at it. You knew this wasn't what I wanted, and you lied to me. I was sixteen!"

I was beside myself. Was this what they'd meant by flight risk? Who was really to blame? Lisa and James or the agency? I was inclined to blame the agency, but maybe the couple was responsible. I wouldn't find out the answer for many years.

I finally hung up the phone, my outrage exhausted, and my world crumbled. I'd been so manipulated! I flashed back to ten years before, the stack of papers I'd signed in the hospital. I remembered signing and signing... asking if I needed to read through them. Brenda had told me no, of course not. I signed so many papers, I was sure they could send me something I had signed. But, we both knew that wasn't what I wanted and that my main stipulation for putting my daughter up for adoption at all was that it was open, for her entire childhood. I had made that abundantly clear. Brenda knew and lied to me about Lisa and James being okay with it, had lied about us all being on the same page, and had lied to me that day when she assured me that I didn't need to read through the paperwork. If I had, I'd have seen all the lies. I wouldn't have signed it; I wouldn't have given Sarah to them.

That would have been Brenda's worst nightmare. After the agency helped me pay for medical treatment and got James and Lisa's hopes up, if I'd balked in the end stage, they couldn't legally force me to give up my baby. Besides, then their lying would have been exposed to James and Lisa as well, which could have made them reconsider using their services.

I cried that day, unable to let go of the phone completely. I felt weak and powerless, having lost control once again. Perhaps all of this had something to do with Sarah's health after all? They might have figured that, without an adulthood to look forward to, they wanted to focus on giving Sarah everything they could during her childhood. Everything except for me.

I wondered if it had to do with the second child they had adopted; if that adoption had presented new challenges to be overcome. Without any concrete information, my mind wandered through all possible combinations and scenarios. Over the years, most of the reasons I could fathom placed the blame squarely on myself. That last small thread that connected me to Sarah had been snipped, unceremoniously, by an uncaring adoption agency in an act that was probably just business.

I had one last opportunity for recourse. One, small, tangible item—a photocopy that held pertinent information that could provide direct access to Lisa and James—access to Sarah. I had tucked it away a few years prior, never anticipating what the future would hold. Which now felt like an answer to a prayer I hadn't even formulated yet. Peace washed over me as I remembered it. I took out the precious box that Lisa had painted for me, a keepsake I'd used to store the letters and pictures, and found the paper. It held everything I'd need to know. Without thinking, I called the number; the first and last time I'd ever do such a stupid thing. I heard a tiny voice answer and hung up abruptly, immediately kicking myself for overstepping. What was I doing? What was my plan?

Part of me thought that it couldn't be real; that the information wouldn't actually lead me to Lisa and James. Or maybe I'd been so taken aback by Brenda's statement that it was reactionary. To prove to myself that I still had some control, even if Lisa and James didn't want to contact me. Whatever the reason, I was disappointed in my loss of control and promised myself that I'd never do it again. It was a promise that I kept.

The next few weeks were beyond difficult. I went through several phases of grief. After a short period of denial, I landed squarely in anger. How could this happen? How was I weak enough to let it happen? What had I done to cause this? Fears and insecurities that I hadn't acknowledged previously now flooded my thoughts. I asked my mom how I could have screwed up so badly, that Lisa and James, people I loved so much, could have rejected me so completely. What could I have done differently? She didn't have any answers for me, but she offered what comfort she could. My dad reminded me how lucky I'd been to already have so much, years of pictures and letters to hold onto and treasure. I assured him that I'd always treasure those. He also told me that I'd be surprised how fast time flies, how Sarah could grow up and, one day, choose to meet me. His words didn't give much comfort, but I appreciated him trying.

I didn't stay in that mental place for long. It wasn't healthy for me or my children. I needed to be healthy and strong for them. Sarah could still be my motivation, just in a more abstract way. One day, she would need me to love and forgive her beloved parents. I couldn't stay angry, couldn't carry that bitterness, because I recognized that neither of those feelings would ever give me joy. Instead, I chose to love unselfishly. To unconditionally forgive them and move forward, both for my own healing and to eventually share my story with others and help them heal too.

This was my new reality, and it was one I'd have to get accustomed to. I had to let go of any hope even for updates—expectations that had been instilled in me by the adoption agency itself. All of that, stripped away. A life without Sarah, no promise of a future, no updates along the way, and not knowing if that girl I passed in the mall was my daughter. My worst fear. All of those things, I had to accept.

She had been my lifeline, the letters and pictures gave me strength when life was hard. It took me a while to realize what I should do then: that I needed to lean on God, my Provider, the one who could bring me ultimate happiness. He had healed me, time and time again. He brought me through difficult challenges in my life, and I knew He would do it again. I reminded myself that if I had truly given Sarah into God's hands when I'd learned about her cystic fibrosis, nothing since then had changed. She remained safely ensconced in His hands. Her parents still held her. She was exactly where she needed to be, protected and loved by her mom, her dad, and her Creator. With Sarah's diagnosis, I had to reach deep within myself to hold onto that. God gave me peace. He gave Sarah life, saved her life, and continued to breathe life into her every day. I had to put one foot in front of the other, content that my own human understanding of the universe didn't matter. What mattered was that God was in control. True faith is only seen when there are no promises or guarantees. I held onto that faith and began making my peace with the new reality.

I began a journey of reflection. I saw that the adoption agency, from the very beginning, never gave me the counseling or guidance to process the emotions or the grief of letting go. I recognized, too, that my childish, careless behavior had led to many undesired outcomes. Blaming others could not bring me the healing I desired; it would only bring more bitterness. If I wanted to move any further, I would need to forgive the people who had hurt me and let me down.

Let me be clear: forgiveness would not be offered as a way of accepting the horrific abuse I had endured. I owed those men nothing. Forgiveness was not an option for the men who had abused their positions of authority and violated my trust in the worst way possible. They deserve nothing. However, for my own peace of mind, I would have to let go of some of that pain. Allowing myself to open my grasp, to not suffer the weight of those heavy, hurtful chains, would be to let joy hold my heart. Joy comes from a deep, tender place. A place of risk and vulnerability. But I knew that this was the right path for me. True joy could not be taken or lessened by my day-to-day disappointments. It was so much bigger than that.

Knowing my decision, I forgave the hurts inflicted by those men, as well as those inflicted by my parents, my church, my own choices, the adoption agency, and my daughter's parents. With that forgiveness came freedom. With that freedom, joy. I was able to find peace within myself, even during that silence, because I knew that, no matter what I wanted for me, Lisa and James were looking out for Sarah.

# ELEVEN

# *Undefined by Silence*

*"My soul, wait silently for God alone, For my expectation is from Him."*
*(Psalm 62:5)*

The next ten years brought me significant growth, maturity, and strength. The adult relationship that I now shared with my mom allowed me guidance, love, and, most importantly, healing. After I'd decided to become a mother, she jumped into her grandmother role with both feet. The love she showed to my children was nothing short of amazing. She and my father helped me immeasurably in those first few years. I took night classes and resigned myself to sleepless nights for homework, challenging myself not to be complacent with welfare and food stamps. During those years, my parents were my rock. They helped watch the kids when I needed time to study. My mom even hired me to work as a preschool teacher, which was truly a godsend. I could bring in my kids, have them looked after, earn an income, and, ultimately, begin my teaching career. I couldn't have known then that this first opportunity would lead to a thirty-year career in the early education field, which still continues today.

As I have shared, throughout the years, God has sent special people into my life, many who have impacted in ways they'll never know. One of these friends was named Sarah. She was a young girl in my preschool class. She'd also been adopted and was only a few years older than my daughter. As the years progressed, she grew up to attend the same church as me. When she was old enough to understand, I told her about my daughter, Sarah, who had been adopted just like her. She was very excited to meet a birth mom, just as excited as I was to know an adopted child. We shared stories and asked each other questions we wouldn't have felt comfortable asking others. It was a unique, special bond. A deep connection, ours and ours alone.

I represented the birth mother she didn't know and she represented the daughter I missed so keenly. Later in her life, Sarah was lucky enough to have the opportunity to reunite with her birth mom. When it happened, she called me immediately, eager to relay the experience. Sarah grew into a young woman and, eventually, a mother herself, and our friendship continued. Sarah invited me to participate in the birth of one of her beautiful daughters, an honor I will always cherish. She frequently asked if I had heard from Sarah yet and encouraged me to not give up hope. She always said that Sarah would want to know me and would love me in return. Our age gap became less and less important the older she got. We will always share a special bond with each other and she gave me some much needed hope.

I was on the right track to success, with my own growing family. The bond that we shared gave me stability, comfort, and a safe haven whenever I needed it. As I had matured, I recognized that I'd be willing to take risks for success. I was willing to make sacrifices others might not have. Although

I initially received some state assistance to get by, I still worked hard at the preschool, worked hard to raise my children, and worked hard to go to college. While finding so many successes, I also faced a new and unexpected loss. When I was married at twenty-one, I imagined it would last a lifetime. I had seen my parent's marriage withstand the test of time. Although I had seen others divorce, it was not something I had imagined for myself. However, after multiple attempts to make it work, our marriage would end in a painful divorce. The impact on the children was my highest priority. I could not have anticipated the trauma and years of grief that would follow; the impact would last a lifetime. At the time, I found myself a single mom once more. Now a mother of three, I was determined to conquer the world! I wouldn't allow societal norms to dictate my life.

After working at the preschool for a several years, and working tirelessly to obtain my Bachelor's, I applied for a job I was certainly not qualified for. Armed with a shiny new degree and ambition that could move mountains, my confidence was high and I felt like I could do anything. Against all odds, I was invited to an interview! The interview was flawless; I had purchased a dark blue power suit and, at the ripe old age of 27, had convinced a panel of professionals that I was the right candidate for the job. My start date was two weeks later. My mom reminded me that I didn't have any professional clothes for the position. I deflated somewhat until she blessed me with $100 and an afternoon of her time. We were determined to find the best deals on professional outfits. Mom suggested a black blazer, which would match with everything, a few signature pieces that I could mix and match, and a few blouses. We had a very successful day. It was fun, exciting, and a fond memory for both of us.

In my new position, I began teaching adults about early education. The opportunity would be a significant step to a successful career. I began writing curricula, developing programs, teaching other teachers, and was soon recognized for my work. I was head-hunted by another vocational school who was willing to hire me with a large pay increase and new responsibilities. Each new aspect was another step on my path. I saw my willingness to take risks really come into play, as well as my ability to say yes to opportunities beyond my experience. My ambition and smarts allowed me to rise quickly.

By 29, I had been sought after by two entrepreneurs, asking me to build a brand-new vocational school in the early education field, hoping to include the entire county! I took full responsibility and created two new locations. I wrote the curriculum, I hired the staff, I designed the interior of the facilities, and developed the whole twelve course training program. I'd never had staff before, nor had I done enough to prepare me for this, but I knew I was capable. My drive propelled me to say "Yes!" and that gave me lots of other opportunities. I started being invited to join Community Boards. Suddenly, my input was valued; I was an active member of the larger community. I began collaborating with other community members. My career took off!

Becoming a single mom again, with three children, was not an ideal situation, but having a solid career helped. I faced the challenges of shared custody, child care, single family income, and loneliness. Even with a house full of children, I would find myself sad and alone. Navigating their emotions and my own would be a challenge. However, I was not going to give up. They were much too important to me. Staying healthy for them was my biggest responsibility. Soon, I faced a brief but difficult obstacle, though I had now learned to use obstacles as launching points for better. California had dropped into a deep financial recession and the schools that I'd been able to create were forced to close. I had to lay off my staff and, ultimately, myself. I remained confident that I could take my years of experience in teaching and developing curricula, with my reputation in the local community, and

188

go teach at the community college. Unfortunately, I was rejected from the job because I didn't have enough education. I had hoped that my BA and experience would be more than enough, but I was wrong. Without a Master's Degree, I did not qualify to teach at the college. I was a bit irritated, but that irritation soon became motivation.

I signed up the following semester to begin my Master's degree in Education. Determined that, whether or not I ever taught at this particular school, I never again wanted to be passed up for a job I knew I could do because I lacked a piece of paper. Fortunately, my parents invited me and my kids to move back in with them while I returned to school.

During that whole time, my journey as a birth mom was simultaneously continuing. For a decade, I believed that I was doing the best I knew how. I followed the rules and expectations to the best of my ability. By nature, I'm a rule-follower, which I demonstrated many times throughout my life. I was hardly without failures—I'm only human—but overall, I lived a life that I could take pride in. I chose to love and respect Sarah's family and put them above my own desires.

In those years of silence, I did my best to keep Sarah real for myself and my family. We began traditions that would last a lifetime. Each year, on Sarah's birthday, I made sure everyone would know. We would all sing happy birthday and pray, both for her and her family. At Christmastime, I placed the white and red booties ornament from 1989 that says "Baby's First Christmas!" Even the kids knew that this was my ornament to hang and allowed me to have the honor of hanging it, front and center on our Christmas tree. On Easter, when we would decorate the eggs together, I'd make an egg just for Sarah, with her name displayed proudly on it. I'd hide it in the garden with all of the others, waiting excitedly for someone to find it. I worked hard to make sure my kids knew their sister, as much as they could. We celebrated her life.

It wasn't just a holiday issue. Sarah was part of my everyday conversation. When people made small talk and asked me how many children I had, I'd respond and add "...and I have another child who I placed for adoption." It never occurred to me to exclude her. To eliminate her from any aspect of my life would erase everything I went through for her and every moment God continued to grant her breath.

Although I often traveled to the LA area for my work, I had never driven past their home. Alia and Kerri often asked me if I did, but the answer was always "no." One day, while traveling with my three children, Daniel asked me where Sarah lived. I told him that I knew her address, but had never visited. He innocently asked if we could drop by and say hi to her. Obviously, that would not happen. I quickly explained that we couldn't do that, that Sarah had a new mommy and daddy and we couldn't go without being invited. Daniel insisted that he wanted to see the house. Initially, I denied his request, not wanting to overstep again. God forbid they might be outside and see me. It'd cause panic for no reason.

However, as I reflected on it, I realized that all of these years, I'd told my kids about Sarah and her new mommy and daddy. They had questions—of course they did. They were curious about the sister they'd never met. I recognized that, by driving by the house, it might bring the kids and me some small closure. It would let us all know that Sarah was not some abstract concept, but a real little girl, growing up somewhere. I decided that we could briefly drive by—what harm could that do? As we got closer to the address, though, my stomach churned. I didn't want to do the wrong thing, a simple drive-by wasn't worth that. I rushed to point out the house.

"Look, you guys! Your sister Sarah is real; she lives in that house, right there. She's alive and well. This is her life."

My children craned their heads a little to peer out the windows at the house I indicated, but I hastened by. We left as quickly as we'd come. I reminded them that when we prayed for her at night, now they knew that she was real. In hindsight, I wish I hadn't done that. Afterwards, it felt like a violation of their privacy. In some ways, it did bring me the peace and closure I'd hoped for, but, in others, it brought me shame. It was easy to make excuses. Why was I the only person who needed to sacrifice their desires for Sarah's welfare? That wasn't who I wanted to be, though. Ultimately, it was harmless, but there had been a risk and I should have chosen differently.

Many people, over the years, have asked me why I didn't just call the house. Why not call Lisa and James to ask them why they'd chosen to cut off all contact? Ask them if Sarah was well. The people who asked me meant no harm in it; they figured that I had the information so why not use it? I was obviously suffering, not knowing. They suggested calls or letters, something that I could send them directly, instead of going through the adoption agency. I did none of those things. When I did occasionally send letters, I sent them to the agency, knowing that they would not be forwarded on. Anything I sent now would be held until a time when or if Sarah became old enough to request them herself.

No, I would continue to respect their family, their privacy, and love them unconditionally. As tempting as direct contact may have been, I couldn't risk the tiny sliver of hope I still carried. The hope that there would be a time when Lisa and James would want me to be a part of their life again, in whatever capacity they chose. I couldn't screw that up. If I did anything to put their guards up around me, I'd be risking that slim chance. I wouldn't risk it. So, I waited, as patiently as I was capable of being.

Although I didn't have any official counseling or therapy for moments like that, I've always been blessed with good friends in my life.

God put people in my life who enabled my healing by giving me guidance and clarity when I needed it the most. One of those individuals is my friend Kim. Kim is a wise, prophetic woman and God speaks to her in deep, wonderful ways. One day, I sat with her and shared how hurt I was to be completely cut out of Sarah's life indefinitely. That her parents no longer wanted a relationship with me in any manner and how worried I was about her illness and uncertain future. She looked at me and responded, with all the confidence in the world:

"Michelle, God has told me something. I see it very clearly: when the tulips bloom, you will be reunited with your daughter."

At the time, I recognized how vague that sounded, but I couldn't help the glimmer of hope it gave me. Despite that, I didn't give the statement much thought in the years that followed. Sometimes, in the back of my mind, I'd remember that promise of a reunion from God, but it was never at the forefront of my thoughts. However, I did use that tiny strand of hope to help me through the crippling absence.

While I continued to gather my bearings from my lay-off and dove deep into my online Master's course, I was invited to live with my aunt, Jennifer. We would have to relocate to Washington. She owned an apartment complex; she would allow my three children and me to have our own place. I would only need to work part-time and could complete my degree. I had never lived out of California before. Leaving behind my parents and my roots would be a huge step of independence. I discussed what moving would mean with the kids and we all agreed it was an adventure worth taking, knowing we could always come home. We packed up our things and began our journey while Kelly Clarkson's song "Breakaway" rang through my head.

We ended up staying in Washington for four years. During that time, I grew both professionally and personally. After completing my Master's, I was hired as the director of a large childcare program. Located on a college campus, I found myself immersed in the two worlds I loved: early education and adult education. I was passionate about advocacy and teaching and my job allowed me to marry those two passions. I wanted to lend my voice to those who could not speak for themselves. In my role as director, I was able to mentor and train my employees while advocating for the needs of children.

It wasn't long before I was asked to transfer to Child Protective Services, a career move which truly demonstrated my compassion for kids and my hope for people to heal. I challenged myself to investigate and document suspicions of child abuse and neglect. I soared in my work. My strength was in my ability to succeed in forensic interviews with young children. I was able to quickly and efficiently build a rapport with them and induce disclosures. I went on to train others in forensic interviewing techniques while I continued to investigate new cases. I immersed myself in my position so completely that my mind and body began to suffer. I saw that the work was unsustainable; the horrific tragedies I witnessed weren't healthy, no matter how much I enjoyed making a difference in people's lives.

As for my personal life, I met a man, much more reserved and quiet than me. I had committed to not dating after my divorce, but he enticed me to make an exception. Adam had never been married before, or a father. He ended up being a risk worth taking, something I reaffirmed a year later when we married. Our wedding was perfect; held on the beautiful backdrop of Lake Stevens, the yard of Adam's childhood home. My family all arranged to be there.

Daniel, now 14, and Jacob, 12, were two of our groomsmen. At the beginning of the ceremony, they led me, one on each arm, as we walked from the house to the wedding aisle. There, they handed me off to my father, to walk me the rest of the way to my awaiting groom. My beautiful 10 year old, Rachel, stood proudly up front as my Maid of Honor. She watched intently, as I demonstrated what a happy marriage could be. I thought of Sarah and wished she could be at my wedding, a dream I'd always had. I was finally confronted with the fact that it would not be so, but the joy of the day overshadowed any sadness. The reality of seeing my mom smile as she watched, hoping that I had found a life-long partner as she had done with dad, brought great happiness. Dad and I would dance to Luther Vandross - Dance With My Father, a moment that would mean even more to me as the years went by.

Although he wanted kids of his own, Adam agreed that if my tubal ligation, which I'd had a decade earlier, could not be reversed, we would live a life together with my beautiful children. Luckily, that didn't end up to be the case. After a successful reversal, I quickly found myself pregnant once again and soon gave birth to our daughter, Lauren. She brought so much joy to our growing family! She connected all of us in ways she wasn't even aware of and we hadn't known we needed.

That same year, Sarah turned eighteen. I had to admit that my father had been right after all when he'd told me how fast the time would fly. I had been anxiously awaiting that critical milestone for Sarah; the age of adulthood and the possibilities it presented. However, I cautioned myself; it could mean nothing. I didn't allow myself to dream too often about a reunion. I prayed and resigned myself to God's will. It was my heart's greatest desire and only wish. When asked what I wanted more than anything, what I wished for when I blew out my birthday candles...it was to see my daughter.

I wondered if now would be the right time to reach out to her. If she might have some interest in meeting me. I contemplated the idea deeply for several weeks, thinking about if or when I should do something. I believed that I had fulfilled my obligation to the adoption and shown enough respect to Lisa and James, but I desperately wanted to contact her. However, her age didn't change my desire to maintain my respect for them, so I decided not to go to Sarah directly. With my complete lack of trust in the adoption agency, I knew I couldn't use them as a platform. It was 2008 and I had Facebook. After spending days settling my nerves, I needed to pull the trigger. To my surprise, my search for Lisa didn't take long. I recognized her beautiful smile immediately, ten years older than I'd last seen her, but as lovely as I remembered. My heart melted at the sight.

Hesitantly, I sent a private message to Lisa, from one mother's heart to another. I hoped for an update, news that Sarah was well, something, anything. But I expected nothing; I couldn't allow myself to hope. It was too painful. Once the message was sent, I stepped away, knowing I had done everything I could. I would wait. Something I had long practiced when it came to Sarah. Luckily, I wouldn't wait too long.

Over the years, with every new move or phone number, I had faithfully contacted the adoption agency. I had to ensure an open line of communication between me, Lisa, James, and Sarah was always available if need be. There would never be a reason why I couldn't be reached. However, I knew that the call I received might be about Sarah's health; that she had been hospitalized or, worse, had passed away. I had to be ready for that as well, though I prayed it would never be the case. I often suffered from a nightmare that would wake me, drenched in sweat. The same terror: that the agency would call to invite me to Sarah's funeral. It felt so real! Sometimes, I would leap from bed, nauseated and in hysterics. Other times, I'd be unable to wake and would suffer the entire nightmare, arriving to find an open casket. Even on paper, I find myself without words to adequately describe that horror.

A few weeks passed after my Facebook message and, without much thought after a long day of work, I opened my mailbox. I had no anticipation of anything other than junk mail and bills. Why should I, after a decade of nothing? I carefully sifted through the junk, my eyes caught the once-familiar return address of the adoption agency. My hands sweated, mind racing. A thousand questions rang out at once in my head. Was I ready for whatever the letter might say? Did I need to prepare for yet another loss, greater than any I'd experienced before? My hands trembled as I stood there, alone on my front porch. I didn't dare enter the house and be delayed by my family's greetings. I needed this moment by myself, undisturbed. I fumbled, trying to hold everything in my shaking hands, and finally opened the letter.

As soon as the paper opened, I saw her, beautiful, grown, and, most importantly, alive. My knees went out and I dropped to the ground. Hard. I dropped everything else in my hands, an uncontrollable weeping coming over me. She was alive. She was alive. I hadn't even realized how sure I'd been that this wouldn't be the case. My doubts were eased and the sobs wracked my body as the adrenaline coursed through my veins. Her gorgeous blue eyes and my smile were there, in my hand. Perfection, exactly as I'd hoped. It looked like she was healthy and living a life with her beautiful family. Rose, the little sister I'd wanted for her was also in the picture, smiling and happy. Rose was an answer to my prayers as well. Seeing her, now eleven years old, made her much more real.

This family, who I loved, was thankfully still intact. Lisa and James were still happily married. I could hardly contain my joy! I sat on the cold concrete for what felt like forever, staring at the pictures. At some point, I realized that I hadn't even read the letter yet! It was from Lisa, explaining how well Sarah was doing considering her illness. She took good care of herself and was very responsible. Her words brought me immense comfort. She shared that Sarah was not yet ready to meet me, but that if and when she was, they would reach out to me. It would have to satisfy, but it was certainly better than the silence. Praise God, I thought, Sarah is well. She is so lovely! My heart overjoyed, I rushed inside. I couldn't wait to share the happy news, to show my kids the pictures of their sister. They were excited to see her after so many years. Part of me hoped that I might receive more letters from Lisa and James after that, but it was not to be.

Life would continue, as it always did. Adam and I knew that we wanted two children together. We jokingly reasoned that, after a $7,000 surgery for reversal, if we had two, each child would only cost half as much. And now, at the age of 36, we couldn't afford to wait long. However, immersed as I was in a career that was taking its toll on my heart, as I intervened into tragic lives, I found my worlds colliding.

On my two year anniversary with Adam, I excitedly gave him his card. I'd bought it a few days earlier, as well as several pregnancy tests. I'd taken one every morning and evening since then and they were all positive. I couldn't wait to tell him! I only saved it because our anniversary was so close. I handed him the card, anxiously awaiting his reaction. He didn't disappoint. Although generally even-tempered, Adam was clearly pleased. We were happy that our family would finally be complete. However, after a couple of weeks, I woke up with cramping blood flowing down my legs. It was a miscarriage. The loss stung deeply. I hadn't even imagined that possibility until it was upon me. The next few months, I buried myself in my work of saving other kids' lives.

Not long after, I happily informed Adam that I was pregnant again. I hoped that the miscarriage had been a fluke and wouldn't happen again. But, a few weeks later, once again, I had a second miscarriage. I was completely devastated. What was happening? Was I too old? Had I already had too many children? Was I doing something wrong? Those questions swirled in my head, combined with grief and fear. I knew how much we wanted one more child. We kept trying and, in total, I suffered four miscarriages. One after another after another. Finally, I realized why.

My heart was so full of passion and love for others, for children and their families. My chest ached when I had to remove kids from their mothers. I could definitely relate to their pain, but I never hesitated to do what was best for the child. I recognized the difference between my story and theirs.

After those four losses, I needed to change directions. I still wanted to continue my work in advocacy and education for children and families, but I also knew that I could do more if I got away from direct service and looked at a role with a broader reach in the early education trajectory. After a call with a friend back in California, I was hired to take a position that would again catapult my life and career into the unknown. After four years in Washington, I was more than happy to return to sunny California. I had missed the weather, my friends, and especially my family. My brother and parents still lived in our small town. However, Adam would stay back for a few months while the older kids finished the school year. Lauren and I went back to visit regularly.

On my last visit, I knew there was something extra that I needed to do. The miscarriages weighed heavily on my heart and I continued to feel that my family was not yet complete. For that visit, after Lauren and I landed, I knew exactly where I should go. I'd heard of the Spokane Healing Rooms; people there will pray for you. I felt sure that, by going there, I would be healed and capable of having a child. My confidence soared as I drove the rented car towards the destination. I'd been thinking about it ever since my brother had told me about them and that Healing Rooms were founded in Spokane. There were plenty of others throughout the country, but this was where it all started. My faith propelled me to go there.

We pulled up, exhausted from a long day of travel. I leaned over to unbuckle Lauren, anxious to go inside. However, as we walked up to the doors, I noticed that it was dark inside. I reached for the door anyway; it was locked. My heart sank. No! I had to go in! I knew, if I could get these prayers, I'd be healed. Despite the locked doors, staring into darkness, I wasn't ready to give up. I recalled the scripture, in Matthew, Chapter Nine. When the sick woman had been bleeding for twelve years, she reached out and simply touched His clothes. When she did so, Jesus said to her: "your faith has healed you." (Verse 22)

So I reached out, again, to the locked door and I asked two-year-old Lauren to reach out as well. As we both held the door handle, I prayed.

"God, just as you healed that woman with her faith, I reach out, now, knowing that you are my healer. I do not need to be inside this building for you to hear my cry. Please, heal my body. Please, bless me with one more child. Amen."

We loaded back into the car, excited to meet up with the rest of our family. That visit, I ended up becoming pregnant with my son. Nine months later, we welcomed Mason into the world. Mason brought a new fulfillment to our full and busy lives. He was a miracle and a true result of my faith. Now raising two girls and three boys, I knew I was done growing my family. My heart and life were full.

My new position quickly grew and I suddenly found myself the CEO of a large non-profit organization, serving children and families in the community in a variety of ways. My hard work in advocacy paid off as I was accepted into leadership roles on local and state boards. No longer held voiceless by loss, I spoke at the State Capitol to State Assembly Members and the Senate. I made individual appointments and advocated at their hearings. I became truly confident in my passions and strengths.

I volunteered for the local pregnancy center, where I was invited to attend classes at the high school—my old high school. I expounded on many topics for students, including: teen pregnancy, depression, rape, adoption, and teen parenting. My life could now be an example to others of what was possible. I advocated for hope and continuously reminded everyone that internal joy is possible, no matter what has happened. I never shied away from telling my story.

People sometimes became awkward when they heard the words "rape" or "sexual abuse," but I never let that stop me. Rape should not be kept a secret. It is not a private matter for the victim and perpetrator alone. It is not a shameful family matter that ought to never be exposed. Rape is a crime and should be punished. I will be sorry forever that I wasn't strong enough, at the time, to pursue legal action against the two men who raped me. However, I have been strong enough to commit to helping others in the years that have followed.

Obviously, I would never have wished to be victimized and raped, but the absolute reality of the situation is I can't take it back. That horrific crime resulted in a beautiful life. God gave me the opportunity to carry one of His children, a life worth saving. He gave me the tools to love unselfishly, to forgive regardless of whether the wrongdoers deserved to be forgiven, and to heal the broken bits inside of me and grow into the woman I have become. For all of that, I am thankful.

# TWELVE

# *Undefined by Tragedy*

*"Then the dust will return to the earth as it was, And the spirit will return to God who gave it." (Ecclesiastes 12:7)*

As my professional life continued to soar, my personal life faced many new heartaches. Raising five children made for a very full and active home. It was a busy time, as both my husband and I worked to balance our lives and support our large family.

The year I turned forty, my life was flipped upside down and would never be the same. I arrived at work planning to swing by my mother's desk to say good morning; nothing seemed amiss. Funnily enough, she had begun working for me at a local non-profit. Talk about a role reversal! I wanted to check in with her because, the night before, she had told us at dinner that she felt weak. She'd nearly dropped a glass of milk, almost as if to punctuate the point. I had hoped that she'd be feeling better after a good night's sleep. Unfortunately, that was not the case.

She still struggled with weakness and, that morning, showed a new symptom as well: confusion. She wasn't herself. Somewhat concerned that I might be overreacting, I drove her to the ER. As I watched her fill out the paperwork for the doctors, my heart sank. Her usual beautiful penmanship was gone, replaced by scribbles. She was quickly rushed into an examination room, ahead of dozens of patients already waiting. Mom had told me not to bother my father; she didn't want to worry him unnecessarily. Despite that, I overheard the doctors bandying words like "diabetes" and "stroke." I knew Dad would need to be involved. I'd spent my whole life learning to respect my parents' wishes, so I struggled with the decision not to obey, but, when they rushed her for an MRI, I called my dad. He'd been taking his usual walk, reminding me once more that today was a day like any other day. I said I'd come get him and he agreed without question. I hustled out to my car, acknowledging to myself that my life would never be the same.

We met outside of the mall and, as we drove, I informed him about mom's serious condition and that she was in the hospital. By the time we arrived, she was coming out of having the MRI. Dad walked in and she responded to seeing him with her familiar, gorgeous smile. I was surprised; why wasn't she upset? It didn't seem like she remembered asking me not to call him. Everything was surreal. Moments later, the machines hooked up to her started beeping and alarms went off. Dad and I were rushed out of the room by medical staff as doctors and nurses bustled in to help. My father and I held each other tightly as we prayed. We had few words, nothing elegant or spiritual, just pleas for God to save her. He heard our cries that day.

My mom went on to have three massive strokes. Each one caused different debilitating conditions, but she lived. Initially, she couldn't walk or talk, and she suffered significant weakness in half of her body. As she healed, she managed to regain most of her essential abilities. After living in rehab for months, she was able to come home. She bore through those challenges with a spirit of determination and continued to improve. Eventually, she was even able to go back to work, on a limited scale.

Just before that return, my oldest son, Daniel, asked to go stay with his Grammy and Papa. At the time, he was twenty-three. I agreed to his request; it would be good for him to be with them, and they could probably use the help. Only a few days later, I received a phone call that turned my world upside down once more. This time, it was my mom's concern: Daniel had fallen asleep and wouldn't wake up.

There'd been a needle in his arm and more in his pockets. I'd had no idea, but, for the past few years, he had an entire secret life suffering drug addiction. I had never personally used drugs, nor had I lived in a family where drugs were ever a concern. I had no idea what I would have been looking for or what behaviors might have tipped me off. I didn't understand; I was so confused. In hindsight, we should have called 911. At the time, I was ignorant; I didn't know how to respond. My fight or flight instincts kicked in. I knew he had to be getting the drugs from somewhere locally so, if I could get him away from the source, I thought he would be okay.

My dad helped me load Daniel's unconscious body into my car. I called my husband and explained that I wouldn't be coming home for a while. I kidnapped my son and fled town. We had no clothes, no food, not even so much as a toothbrush. I drove north, with no destination in mind, trying to get as far away as I could. Daniel hardly stirred. As night fell, I belatedly realized that I was near my Aunt Jennifer, who now lived in the Bay Area. I called her and told her the situation. She recommended a nearby hotel and agreed to help in any way possible. I spent that night, and many nights after, with Daniel in that hotel room. I kept him there and did my best to keep him alive as he hallucinated and threw up—the symptoms of massive and sudden withdrawal. Aunt Jennifer brought us food and some essential things, enough to sustain us. Other than that, we had no contact with the outside world.

He spent a lot of time sleeping. I would hold his shaking body and pray. I didn't know the extent of what was happening; it'd take me years to learn the whole story. However, this stay was the beginning of both his road to recovery and his long journey battling addiction. On the third night, he finally mustered a bit of an appetite as his body fought to regain control. On my fortieth birthday, we walked next door to Denny's for dinner. There was nowhere I'd rather be than with my son, doing everything I knew how to help him. The next day, the anxiety crept in. He wanted to leave the room, the addiction driving him to seek out a new source. Even when he pleaded with me for fresh air, I refused. I finally issued an ultimatum: turn yourself in to Teen Challenge, an in-patient drug rehabilitation program, or be left here, wherever here was, homeless and without money.

He tried to tell me that I was overreacting; he didn't have a problem, I did. He could stop any time he wanted. Even then, I knew it was an act. I might not have known much about drugs or addiction, but I knew he couldn't control it on his own; he needed help. I didn't yield. He had his two choices. I stood absolute. I would leave him there, alone, in Northern California. He'd have to fend for himself. Or, I would give him a ride to Teen Challenge, where he'd have a bed to sleep in, food to eat, and whatever he needed to heal. He begged me for a third option; to let him come home and live with me again. He promised he'd stop using. No matter how much I wanted to believe him, to agree, I knew I didn't have the training or resources to help him. I wanted him to go somewhere with people who knew what they were doing. Although extremely reluctant, I finally persuaded him to go.

We drove the three hours towards Teen Challenge. At one point, he yelled that he'd changed his mind.

"No way I'll go there!"

I calmly pulled over, stopped the car, unlocked the doors, and told him to get out. He stared back at me, disbelieving. I leaned over him and opened the door. His beautiful blue eyes were hardly recognizable anymore.

"But, it's not even safe out there!"

Part of me wanted to laugh. He was already killing himself with the drugs, what did it matter where he walked? He pleaded with me to close the door, not to make him do this. I held fast to my conviction.

"I will not bring you home just to watch you die from an overdose. I have seen too much in my life and this time, it's my choice. I will not watch my son die in our home. I won't do it! This is your one opportunity. What are you going to do?"

In the end, he agreed to go. We'd spent four nights together when we finally arrived at Teen Challenge. The counselors came out to greet us, and I nearly sank to the ground with relief. It wasn't all on me anymore. I wasn't alone, trying desperately to hold everything together. They greeted Daniel with a hug and assured me that he'd be safe there. That I could go without worry; they had it handled from here. We prayed together, and I eventually climbed back into my car. I paused before starting it and gripped the steering wheel tightly, resting my forehead against my hands. I was overwhelmed with relief, fear, and confusion. I tried to start my drive home, but only made it about a mile before my tears came hard enough that I had to pull over. I wept in my car, feeling the weight of the world on my shoulders. Now that Daniel was no longer relying on me and I was alone, it paralyzed me.

My crying was abruptly interrupted by my ringtone. It was my son, Jacob. He'd been away for months, in the Army, and I hadn't spoken to him in weeks. Hearing his voice right then was amazing. My joy was dampened somewhat by my own exhaustion, but I was desperate for his beloved voice.

"Hey, Mom. What are you doing tomorrow?"

I hadn't been home in days. I hadn't even showered for fear that Daniel would have used the opportunity to sneak out and get high again. I was tired, filthy, and missed my family. I'd been absent from work, and I wasn't even sure I knew what day it was! I gathered my thoughts and assured him I'd be home, hoping we could see each other.

"Yeah, of course! Can you come to my wedding at the courthouse tomorrow?"

What? Wedding? That was big news! He was only twenty-one, and I hadn't seen him in so long. I was obviously out of the loop. Nevertheless, I promised him I'd be there. I was so tired; I could barely comprehend the weight of the conversation. I wiped the tears away from my face where I noticed they were still running and tried to sound focused. I wanted to convey my excitement for this new adventure.

With every last bit of energy, I drove the three hours home. I arrived late into the night and immediately headed for the shower. I stood there, head tipped back, and let the hot water gush down my body, soaking my hair. I took a deep breath, then another, then another one. I had to prepare myself for the wedding, only hours in my future, but right then, in that shower, I took a moment for Michelle. Of course, I was completely committed to being present for my son. For all of my children. I wanted to support Jacob's decision and show him the time and attention that he so richly deserved. But, right then, I also thought about Daniel. Agonized over whether he'd turned to drugs because he had needed something I hadn't given him, what signs I'd missed, what preventative measures I could have taken. I questioned, however briefly, whether I'd made the right decision with Daniel, now knowing he'd miss his brother's wedding. I allowed myself those doubts and guilt, but firmly took my emotions in hand when I toweled off.

The next morning, we all got ready for the wedding. My parents came with us when we drove to the courthouse. I was thrilled to embrace Jacob. The Army had made him a man in the time since I'd last seen him, and I couldn't have been more proud. We occupied ourselves with taking some family photos while we waited our turn. We tried to enjoy what time we had because he was due to leave for another year overseas in only two weeks.

After the short ceremony, we all shared brunch. My elation began to be overshadowed by my renewed exhaustion and I felt pressure to return to the office since I'd been gone for nearly an entire week. I fought all of that to stay present and in the moment. During the brunch, my mom quietly asked if I'd mind coming over.

"Daniel left a mess in the garage."

Fresh guilt washed over me. I felt terrible about that; my mom didn't need to be bothered tidying up after my son. She was still healing; this ought to be the least of her concerns. I assured her I'd come and clean it up. After the brunch, we said our goodbyes and I wasted no time changing my outfit and heading over to my parents' house. I wanted to get it done quickly so I could still make it into the office. Nothing prepared me for the sight of their garage; it'd been turned into a meth lab. Again, my ignorance worked against me. Disassembling the equipment was extremely dangerous. I should have called professionals to do it; I easily could have blown up myself and the house. But, I didn't know, so I jumped into high gear and tackled the whole project on my own. I loaded up enormous black trash bags, continuously shocked by what I found in there.

A few hours later, I rushed to check in at my office. After a week away, there was a lot of catching up to do. I waited for my computer to boot up, anxious to get in some work before the end of the day. It seemed like only moments later when a coworker asked if I was leaving soon. I giggled, telling him I'd only just got to work. I needed to at least read up on all of my emails. He gave me a strange look.

"Michelle, you've been sitting there, staring at your screen for hours. You haven't been moving, reading, or typing."

I laughed nervously, sure that he was joking. I'd just turned my computer on; it was still loading! However, when I looked up at the clock, I saw the truth: three hours had passed. A memory from years ago, while I was still pregnant with Sarah, flashed through my mind. I remembered driving home from LA and feeling as though I'd been transported. I'd lost time, though there were no sunflower seeds as proof this time. The strain of the psychological stress had, once again, surprised me. My coworker, and the clock, were proof enough. He sat directly behind me; he'd have seen my inactivity. My body, mind, and soul were beaten. I hung my head, knowing I needed rest, comfort, and healing. Sadly, life wasn't ready to give me that time. Tragedy struck again.

In March of 2014, I called my father on his 69th birthday. I wished him all the best, but it was obvious that something was wrong. He said he didn't feel well. I suggested rest, thinking about how I needed the same, and promised to call back to check on him later. Except that, later, he didn't answer the phone. I picked up my mom from work, worried about not getting a response, and we drove to their house to see for ourselves what had happened. Through the living room window we saw him resting on the couch. We knocked at the door, but there was no answer. Finally, he woke up and came to unlock the door. At first, it seemed like the rest had done the trick, but then he collapsed, unable to hold up the weight of his own body.

As he attempted to crawl to the couch, skin gray, I was frozen. The sight shook me to the core. I asked him repeatedly what was wrong, kneeling down next to him, trying to help him maneuver. He didn't know. We were both terrified. I vacillated between trying to help him to the couch and running for the phone. In the end, I called 911, and he was rushed to the hospital. We were all shocked to find out that his sickness wasn't recent; he'd likely been sick for over twenty years. Leukemia. I barely comprehended the diagnosis. How could my father, the strongest man I knew, have been so sick for so long? How had none of us noticed? He'd been my rock for my entire life, I couldn't fathom that he'd been fighting his own battle the whole time. I hardly had time to process the doctor's information; three short weeks after receiving the devastating news, my father passed away.

This tragedy would easily be marked as the greatest loss in my life thus far. During the first several months, I worked hard to take my father's place as the strong one, for my mom and my grandmother. They'd lost their husband and son. I couldn't begin to imagine their pain. I helped in all the ways I knew how. However, after a few slight indications that they'd begun to heal, I found myself falling into a deep, dark depression. It was the same, in some ways, to what I'd experienced after having Sarah. I desperately tried to regain control in my life, using food as a means to control what I could. Everything had started spiraling out of control, and I wanted to have my choices matter. After Sarah, I exercised maniacally and refused to eat. After my father, I overate.

I gained weight quickly. Everything about my lifestyle was unhealthy, mentally, physically, and spiritually. The depression took over my entire world. All of my hope had been shattered with his loss. My day-to-day life felt empty and out of sync. This wasn't something I could take charge of, something I could fix on my own. For the past 25 years, while enduring grief and loss through adoption, I still held onto God's promises of my future. My hope for a future with my daughter. I watched God give His blessings and healing to Rachel in my womb, my mom, helping her survive her strokes, and with Daniel's drug addiction. I saw God intercede and give me insight and strength when I felt unsure. My father's death was so much more final. He was just...gone.

There was nothing to change, nothing to do, nothing to give insight about, no decisions to be made. Nothing I could say or do would change the finality of death. My mom ached with the loss of her lifelong companion, the man that she loved. My grandmother ached with the loss of her oldest son, her baby boy. I knew what it was like to fear for the life of your child, but, even in my wildest nightmares, I couldn't fathom the sorrowful depths of anguish that would come from truly losing your baby. I keenly felt their grief in addition to my own. I didn't know how to move forward. Part of me didn't think I deserved to feel that sorrow to the same extent as them. I always knew I'd outlive my father; it's the natural order of things. No one should have to outlive their child or their lover. I didn't have the strength to pray for my own healing. I was in a dark pit, a hollowed-out shell of my former self.

In another example of God's infinite wisdom, that He'd shown time and time again, He brought a very special family into my life at the perfect time. A couple from my church, Mike and Jennifer, and their beautiful young daughter Michaela. March of 2014 was a time of shared grief, for both of our families. That grief drew us together. Just days after my father entered the hospital, Jennifer's mother passed away. Her father followed, two days later, and then I lost my own dad. Together, we suffered unimaginable sorrow.

In the weeks, months, and years that followed, our grief bound us in ways we hadn't known we needed. We stayed strong for each other, even in the face of our terrible losses. We wrapped our arms around each other on Father's Day and cried in tandem on Mother's Day. We shared a gift of understanding, the depths of which we couldn't have foreseen. Our friendship withstood the test of time. Years later, we've created traditions and family celebrations of our own, linking our lives together forever.

A year after my father's passing, I looked down at myself, seemingly for the first time in a long while. My body so much heavier than I remembered it being. I'd gained thirty pounds when I wasn't looking. My heart was broken, unhappy, and lacking motivation. I had no passion or creativity. I wasn't excited about life. I knew better than that. I had so much to live for, both family and friendships! I couldn't keep wallowing in my own misery forever and waste my life. What had I done to myself? What was I still doing? At that moment, I experienced something I never thought I'd feel: I was not ready to meet Sarah. Since her adoption, it was all that I ever dreamed about, but, now, I wasn't living a life she could be proud of. I needed her approval. I wanted her to be honored to have my genetic lineage, but, mostly, I wanted her to love me as much as I have always loved her.

When I finally saw myself with some clarity, I knew I was not the person I had spent so much time and worked so hard to be. If she called me that day, if she had reached out to me, I couldn't honestly tell her I was ready. I couldn't give her the healthy, strong, and whole woman I wanted to be. That day, I made an important decision. I had to turn my life around. I would get healthy physically, mentally, and spiritually. I would ask God to forgive and heal me, as He had faithfully done so many times before.

I knew I couldn't get better overnight. It would need to start with small steps. I asked God to help me take steps towards my healing. I wanted to find my motivation, my passion, my ultimate joy. These baby steps forward would send me on a positive trajectory toward a healthy and steady growth. I later came up with an acronym for this process: TINY, Transform Intentionally = New You! Those tiny, intentional steps led to change in a HUGE way. Helping U Get Everything! I began working on those steps each day to improve my life. Simple things like doing a ten-second wall squat while I brushed my teeth, or waking up fifteen minutes early for some time alone that I could use for prayer.

Much like what I did to prepare for Sarah's adoption, in those last weeks of pregnancy, so many years ago, I once more committed myself to intentionally taking steps forward in my thinking and actions to get to a positive end result. Over the years, I had to learn to take these TINY steps and learn to let go. After Sarah, I had to let go many more times. This lesson was the tool that propelled me to healing, time and time again.

When Daniel was born, I let go of my own childish and irresponsible ways. When I lost my unborn babies, I let go of the pain that could have swallowed me whole. When I divorced, I let go of the dream that I had created a picture perfect family. When Jacob joined the Army, I let go of my dreams for his life, and allowed him to follow his own. When I dropped Daniel off at Teen Challenge, I let go of control to let another help. Now, faced with the death of my father, I knew it was time to let go. To find the peace that my heart needed to heal. It would start TINY and grow into HUGE change.

Within four months, I had lost thirty pounds. I started to notice the sunrise again, its warmth on my skin. One day, as I walked into my house robotically after a long day of work, Mason and Lauren, my two youngest, came to greet me. They were eager to see me, anxious to share the news of their day. As I gazed into their smiling faces, I felt as though I saw them clearly for the first time in many months. I glanced around my home. It should have been familiar, but, strangely, it wasn't. I observed how clean it was, though I had no memory of cleaning it. The past year felt like a dream, one that I was finally waking up from and hardly remembered.

I hugged the kids, crying. I had finally broken free from the dark chains of my grief. That horrible anguish was behind me, and I could begin to heal. I had reached the next level of joy. I wanted to get better, not just for my family, for my father's memory, but for me. I wanted to be ready, if Sarah ever reached out. I had people who needed me and, for all of them, I wanted to find myself again. When I changed that mindset, my behavior soon followed. Soon, I was able to turn around the self-sabotaging behaviors and gain control of my life in a healthy, productive way. I was so grateful that God had taught me a simple principle I could use to succeed in life. It's a practice I continue to use every day.

The following year, I continued to move forward. I took Sarah and my father with me in my daily life. Not a day passed that I didn't think of both of them, that I didn't pray. They were a big part of me and thinking of them often helped me in my journey to heal. I spoke about my dad, my grief at his passing, the joyful times we'd had together, and, ultimately, how much I missed him. I didn't shy away from sharing my grief because it helped to talk about it; Jennifer always listened and completely understood. Despite my new mindset and determination, life was still far from perfect or simple.

Daniel was in year two of drug rehabilitation, a program that would last for seven years. Jacob was deployed overseas again after a painful divorce, so soon after I'd attended his courthouse wedding. My mom was still working to regain her health after the strokes and my father's death. I still had three children at home, and I needed to balance them, my husband, and a demanding career. However, I took solace in the fact that I walked in

God's grace and protection. I had faith that, eventually, taking TINY steps would lead me towards HUGE success.

March 4, 2016. I was walking through Costco with my daughter, Rachel. It was no different from any other day we'd gone shopping. We casually browsed the store that evening, with no specific mission in mind, and made small talk. Over to my left, I caught a glimpse of a large portable shelving unit, covered in simply planted bulbs. I noticed that they were tulips. Suddenly, I couldn't catch my breath. I gulped repeatedly.

"Tulips, tulips, tulips…"

The only word I could think circling around and around in my head. Nothing came out of my mouth and I struggled to breathe. I'd seen tulips in bloom every year, my whole life, and never had I been so overwhelmed by the sight of them. For some reason, when I saw the tulips that night, I was flooded with the memory of Kim, telling me about God's promise, so many years ago.

"When the tulips bloom, you will be reunited with your daughter."

I stumbled towards the tulips, in a trance of some sort, my heart pounding. Sobs erupted from my lips as I got closer. Rachel immediately ran over and took my arm, looking frantic.

"What is it? What's wrong?"

I had never told her about the tulip prophecy. I'd never told anyone. In fact, I'd barely thought about it for years. Abruptly, it was all I could think about. I explained it haltingly to Rachel, and she seemed excited about the hope it promised. Wiping away my tears, we continued through the store while I ducked my head. I couldn't believe I'd just broken down in the middle of Costco of all places! I giggled a little bit, elation swelling in my chest. Something was different; I felt it in my bones. I didn't know what it was, but I was certain that something had changed.

The next day would have been my father's 71st birthday. A day that had once been filled with such happiness for us had now been soured as the beginning of the end. Rachel and I sat on the couch as I told her how bitter I was that this day, of all days, could have been tainted. I didn't want to do anything. I sat, despairingly, not fully retreating back into my depression, but recognizing the day my father had been rushed to the hospital, heralding his death. I barely paid attention to what was on the TV. I had my phone out, browsing social media, and texting on and off with my friend, Sarah. Suddenly, I received a notification that would change my life. My daughter had found me!

Did she know who I was? Was it an accident? I couldn't ask; I was petrified. What if she hadn't meant to do this? Rachel leaned over and, seeing what was happening, reassured me that I should respond. I froze. I texted my friend, Sarah, since she'd been so encouraging over the years about me reaching out to my daughter. She also insisted that I should respond. They both encouraged me to return the message, but my fear held me back. I didn't know what to do. After an hour, I began to process the event and began to contemplate the risk. I'd waited a lifetime; I wasn't willing to risk it all. But maybe I should have? My sweaty hands trembled around my phone and I thought about my reaction to the tulips the night before. I recognized the significance of that, as well as my father's birthday. God was giving me so many signs!

With all of my anticipation, fears, and hopes brimming, I typed back: Do you know who I am?

Her response was prompt: Of course. Of course! Of course!

I squealed like a little girl and leapt up from the couch. Adrenaline pumped through my veins, overtaking the boredom and gloom I'd been suffering only an hour ago. She knew it was me, knew who I was, and still had reached out. I tore through the house, searching for other family members, tripping over my words to explain what had happened. I barely managed to communicate the basic idea. Sarah wanted to talk to me! I called my mom immediately, anxious to share this amazing moment with her. I knew she'd be overjoyed as well. She'd been a part of this journey, right there with me, suffering her own pain of giving up her first grandchild. I was right; she was so happy for me!

I told her how the day had been so sad, but could now be celebrated. March 5th, a day redeemed by God and Sarah! My friend, Sarah, and Rachel were equally elated. The messages continued, back and forth, for over an hour. Later that day, I reached out to Kerri and Alia, both of whom couldn't contain their excitement either. I deeply wished that I could call my dad and tell him the great news, but, somehow, I felt that he already knew.

In the weeks that followed, Sarah and I continued to message each other. I told Sarah that this would be on her terms, she'd be calling all of the shots. I'd follow her lead. I didn't want anything to make her uncomfortable. She told me that she was married, told me about her husband, Tom, and the love they shared. She admitted that they'd married quite quickly after a short engagement because they'd wanted to hurry up and spend the rest of their lives together. After a few weeks of us getting to know each other, Sarah gave me her cell phone number and we moved on to texting every day. We shared our likes and dislikes, our silly habits, and discovered our common interests. It turned out that we actually had quite a lot in common! Both of us enjoyed following the rules and pleasing others. We had some nearly obsessive compulsions, like counting items and assigning inanimate objects a random gender. We laughed at our shared ridiculousness and so much more.

We had the same dry sense of humor and a strong sense of responsibility about life. We both expressed our total commitment to loving Christ, which, of course, brought me great joy to hear. One day, while we were discussing our love of Coca Cola, Sarah casually told me that she'd always known that I loved her. My heart skipped a beat. She always knew... my lifelong prayer had been heard by God! It had been delivered by James and Lisa, heard and believed by Sarah. Nothing else mattered. Not the mistakes of the adoption agency, not my insecurities about Lisa and James, nothing. They'd been faithful to their promise to share my love with her. With those simple words, my life felt complete. I finally had everything I'd ever dreamed of. Anything beyond that would be blessings overflowing.

During the next few months, Sarah and I shared many stories about our respective lives. We sent pictures and videos of emotional or funny moments and followed each other on social media. Not a day went by that we didn't connect in some new way. It might be something like a quick picture of our favorite treat: French fries and coke, or we'd spent hours discussing the deep thoughts of life, religion, politics, and family. One thing we bonded over, in particular, was her desire to have a baby. She wanted to know everything about my pregnancies! It was a topic I never minded talking about, especially my pregnancy with her.

I hadn't missed the way that most people became awkward when I discussed Sarah or my pregnancy. Even while I was pregnant with my other children, if I mentioned Sarah, they'd usually shut down or change the topic. It was safe to talk about my other pregnancies, children, even labor and delivery, but with Sarah, they seemed eager to move on to other conversations. I didn't recognize it consciously, but I was aware. When Sarah started asking for details, I realized that I hadn't thought about those details in a long while, having gotten used to not sharing them as openly. I'd have to search deep in my brain for those memories. The second thing

I realized was that it was fun! I could finally discuss the stories of that time with someone who wasn't politely listening, but actually wanted to know. I found the process invigorating.

The memories flooded my heart, the good and the bad, all raw and authentic. I enjoyed telling Sarah about the weird food cravings she'd given me, the terrible bouts of morning sickness. She wanted more! How many weeks had I gone before it started? When I told her about the OJ sardine ice pops, she pretended to gag, totally grossed out. I told her about needing Taco Bell with extra sour cream every day. I apologized for all of the soda that I'd drunk; clearly the caffeine cravings were still strong in both of us!

Despite our mostly light-hearted talks, I needed to know about her health. How was her life with cystic fibrosis? How had it impacted her over the years? How would it impact her future? I had so many questions, but I was cautious about overwhelming her. I wanted to make sure we stayed within her comfort zone. It took some time, but Sarah eventually opened up about some of her experiences. Doctors had theorized that she wouldn't live much past thirteen. She'd had several hospitalizations over the years, but the most serious one had happened when she was nineteen.

During that time, the prognosis had been dire; her family had been told to prepare themselves because she wouldn't survive. Lisa, however, refused to give up. She began a desperate search for the best doctors, the best medicine she could find. Lisa had prayed diligently to the God she loved and relied on that He would save Sarah. Once again, Lisa proved that God had chosen her maternal role well. She was eventually successful when she found a new hospital that had doctors who specialized in cystic fibrosis and Sarah had a miraculous recovery. Now 26, Sarah had survived and wanted to become a mother herself. The doctors understood her desires and didn't discourage her from trying. We spent many hours talking over the possibilities, what pregnancy was like, even tips and tricks too embarrassing to mention.

One day, I suggested that she buy some ovulation tests from the dollar store. She felt a little embarrassed and demurred. Without telling her, I went to the store and bought 100 tests, a mixture of ovulation and pregnancy tests. I sat in front of the TV that night and tediously began wrapping each one. I smiled with each completed box. I felt such joy; joy in preparing my first gift for my daughter. Joy that we finally had a relationship. Joy in the silliness of individually wrapping a hundred little boxes. I told her I had a present and asked where she'd want me to mail it. Without hesitation, she gave me her address. Two days later, I received photos of her opening the gift. I laughed at the idea of her unwrapping every single one and the images captured her own laughter. I liked the idea that maybe Tom was taking the pictures, thinking about how silly both of us are.

Ironically, despite all of our communications, not once had we actually spoken. All of our messages had been text and pictures. I didn't know my own daughter's voice. I imagined what it would sound like, and tried to anticipate her tone. The texts made her emotions clear so I pretended that I could hear her inflections, her sarcasm, her humor, or her sadness. For nine months, we continued to build our relationship, the tentativeness slowly fading from our interactions.

During that time, I continued building a solid career in early education, but I still had a desire I hadn't yet fulfilled. The local community college that had once turned me away due to lack of education now asked me to partner with them during my other jobs. While on a break at a partnership meeting, I casually mentioned my lifetime desire to teach there. That I'd been a student many years before and had always wanted to be a professor one day. Although it was intended to be casual conversation, it quickly turned serious when they informed me that I could look into that kind of opportunity now.

Not only was that available to me, but they would love for me to consider it. I knew I wouldn't leave my current job as CEO, but I could add something part-time. After getting through the HR process, I was officially offered a position. I was really excited to begin teaching early childhood education to young adults. The class was perfect for me. Childhood Development covered everything from conception through adolescence. By then, I'd had a lifetime of experience, particularly with pregnancy. As always, I never held back when sharing my personal stories; the ones that supported my efforts towards education. My students embraced me and enjoyed my teaching style. I started by telling them that, twenty years prior, I'd sat in their seats and leaned over to the person next to me, saying that, one day, I'd teach there.

I loved telling Sarah about my lectures, and she loved hearing about them. That's when she told me about sending me a message on Facebook, in January of 2015, more than a year before we'd reconnected. I was shocked to hear that! She'd reached out, interested to know me, that long ago? I couldn't believe it! I'd certainly never received that message! I'd waited her whole life for that opportunity, no way I'd have squandered it so carelessly. She sent me a screenshot of the original message and told me that she'd resent it when I initially hadn't responded. I searched my Facebook, anxious to see how I could have possibly missed such an important message. It wasn't there! It made no sense. It didn't matter anymore, but we were completely baffled at how it could have happened. I felt a little sick; I'd missed an entire year that I could have spent with her. Obviously, I'd have to let it go, but it shocked me and I hurried to reassure her that I never saw it.

She agreed and told me she'd been surprised that I hadn't responded. She'd assumed I wouldn't hesitate. When I hadn't said anything, she was confused and disappointed. My heart panged in sympathy, but there was nothing I could do. I was just happy that she believed me when I told her I'd never received it. Apparently, part of her had assumed that, even back then. She'd always been confident that, if I'd seen it, I would have wanted to know her. That wasn't the last time she'd surprise me with a message, though. She once again shocked me to the core when, on my 44th birthday, she texted to wish me a happy birthday and offered me the greatest gift I could ever receive. She wanted to meet me in person.

I stared down at the text, my heart rabbiting inside my chest. I never thought that I could feel greater joy than when Sarah reached out to me. Her contact in my phone had been, "New Joy Sarah," since the day she'd shared her number with me. The joy I'd felt while we'd bonded was larger than anything I had ever imagined. It came from a place so deep, vulnerable, and wrapped in a mixture of hope and anticipation. It never occurred to me that I could feel an even greater joy. Yet, as I continued to run my fingers over the words on my phone's screen, I truly felt as if I'd ascended. My answer, of course, was "YES!" but it took me a little while to steady my hands enough to type the words. It'll always be "yes" for Sarah.

I'd become pregnant with Sarah in March and delivered her in December. Twenty-seven years later, we reconnected in March and she gave me the gift of reunion nine months later, in December. The past five years of my life had been very hard, but now, I felt the reward of pushing through those hardships. We quickly began planning our meet-up. We wanted to wait until after the holidays. We planned for January but, just days before she was due to arrive, a family emergency delayed her trip. She felt terrible about cancelling; she didn't want me to take it personally or think that she was just making an excuse because she'd changed her mind about wanting to meet me. She was obviously concerned, but I told her that it didn't matter. Her family came first. We could easily reschedule; she needed to be with them now. I meant it, too.

For me, whether it happened now or far in the future, the very fact that Sarah wanted to meet me was absolutely enough. She said it would happen and I believed her. I had no doubts. The delay meant nothing, I only hoped that her family would be okay. I prayed for Lisa, James, Rose, Tom, and Sarah. I considered them my family too. It turned out, I wouldn't have to wait long for our meeting anyway. Another month passed and we rescheduled. It was now February of 2017.

When the week arrived, we'd already spent so many hours texting. I felt like we knew each other so well. I had always been willing to be real with her and it seemed like there was nothing we couldn't say to each other. I was completely open and honest with her in every conversation. We often talked about places we'd been. We'd ask whether the other one had been there too. If we'd been at the same place at the same time, maybe passed each other on a freeway or in a mall? I told her about looking into the eyes of strangers I walked by, trying to find her.

The anticipation grew stronger with every passing day. I kept asking myself: is this real? Am I dreaming? I'd been imagining this moment for 27 years. Could it really be my dream come true? It was hard to organize all of my thoughts. I began cleaning everything—my cupboards and closets, my garage and art supplies. I organized junk drawers and went through all of my children's special possessions. I sorted and cleaned those too. I was too motivated and inspired to sleep. I felt truly fulfilled, honored by God.

When I told my friend, Jill, about all of the cleaning and organizing, things like my sock drawer that Sarah wouldn't even notice, Jill smiled widely. She happily told me that it sounded like I was nesting. We cried with happiness and took a moment to feel the significance of everything together.

A few days before Sarah would arrive, I walked through a clothing store with Jill. I wanted something new to meet Sarah. I texted her as I walked, telling her what I was up to and how I daydreamed about our reunion. I planned to hear her voice and embrace her immediately. As I stood, admiring a blouse, I noticed a woman standing next to me. I couldn't stop myself from engaging her in conversation. I told her that I was looking for the right outfit to meet my birth daughter for the first time. She smiled awkwardly at me, but I didn't care. I was firmly on Cloud Nine. As I approached the checkout counter, five perfect outfits neatly folded in my cart, my phone alerted me with a notification. I was surprised to see that it was from Facebook; I thought I'd turned those off. The message was from Sarah. That was no shock, but when I opened it up, I nearly fumbled my phone.

It was the message from 2015! Two years later, there it sat, innocently, at the top of my private messages. How did this happen? I knew it couldn't be possible. I stepped out of line to find Jill and immediately messaged Sarah, sending her a screenshot of it. There was nothing logical about it. Jill and I stared at it intently, thinking I must have somehow missed it before. But there it was, unread, as a new notification. As we climbed into the car, I reflected on when Sarah had sent the message. I explained to Jill, it had been the only time in my life that I hadn't been ready to meet her. The one time in my life that she wouldn't have been proud of me because I wasn't proud of me. I knew this had to be God's work. He always knew and He'd waited, wanting to send the message on His time. I realized that Sarah wasn't the one calling the shots. It wasn't her, or me, or Lisa and James, or my parents...it was God. This visit was truly His doing and His timing in bringing us together.

This reunion was bigger than either of us would know. The powerful connection that God had created between us was evident. A story we shared that was worth telling. We could bring hope and healing to so many others. I knew this story needed to be told. I was living the story. That moment imprinted in my mind as part of the miracle of our intertwined lives, and I wanted to share it with the thousands of people God would help heal. This was so much larger than Sarah or me, I just didn't know how yet.

The night before Sarah came, Jill invited me to a girl's night out in celebration of her birthday. We went to the Great American Melodrama in Oceano, about 25 minutes away. I was so happy to be out that night; there was nothing left to clean and I couldn't focus. My mind was solely on tomorrow. I would meet Sarah and her husband. Tomorrow, my life would change forever, my prayers finally answered. I couldn't suppress the excitement! I kept sending Sarah texts about it, eager to see her. She responded in kind. I couldn't say what the show was about, I couldn't pay attention to Jill or the show. I found myself smiling, alone in the dark.

When the break arrived and the lights came up, as is tradition there, one of the actors called out birthdays and anniversaries so the audience could sing for the people celebrating. I raised my hand for Jill, something I'm sure she didn't appreciate. The host asked her for her name and age and we all sang "Happy Birthday" to her and six other guests. After that, the host asked for couples who were there for their anniversary. A couple to my left raised their hands and they gave their names as James and Lisa. That caught my attention and I glanced over at them. I snorted, obviously there were other couples named James and Lisa. I told Jill about the weird coincidence. I definitely had Sarah on the brain that night!

I went to text Sarah about it, but the lights went down and the performance resumed. I was anxious to get home and go to sleep, like a kid on Christmas Eve. I wanted the next day to hurry up and come! I couldn't sleep. I kept checking the clock every few minutes, checking the rest of the house for the tiniest speck of dust I could remove. There was nothing, of course. I looked at the pictures adorning my walls. Were they hung straight? Should I adjust them? I wondered if Sarah was able to sleep.

# THIRTEEN

# *Defined by Love*

*"Love suffers long and is kind; love does not envy; love does not parade itself, is not puffed up; does not behave rudely, does not seek its own, is not provoked, thinks no evil; does not rejoice in iniquity, but rejoices in the truth; bears all things, believes all things, hopes all things, endures all things." (1 Corinthians13:4-7)*

The day had finally arrived! I'd been waiting for more than half my life for this day, been dreaming about it, had been kept awake by thoughts of what would happen...The day I'd fallen asleep in front of the TV to avoid thinking about it. Despite all of my imaginings, that day, everything slotted perfectly into place. It felt right. God's timing was impeccable. When she came, we'd planned a short road trip to San Luis Obispo. We wanted to amble around the town, just the four of us. Rachel wanted to meet her sister and had agreed to come with us. Then, we'd all come back for a homemade dinner. I was so excited; I'd get to cook my first dinner for my daughter. We both knew how special the day would be and had talked extensively about it. Much like the day in the hospital after she'd been born, there was no place I'd rather be. This was our special moment.

In the years we'd been apart, I would often see beautiful reunions between long estranged people on TV. I thought about the day Oprah would contact me and want to hear about Sarah and my amazing story. My imagination went even further to daydream about being on her show and the surprise I'd feel when Sarah walked out to greet me. Childhood imaginings that never faded as I aged. But, now, finally, it was happening. No fanfare, no lights, no cameras, no audience to cry along with us. It would be intimate and perfect. I know Sarah was looking forward to that too.

The hours seemed to drag by as I waited for Tom and Sarah's arrival, but even that didn't matter. Nothing could bring down my mood! I was almost as excited to meet Tom; I wanted to know what Sarah loved about him, what kind of man my daughter decided to marry. Sarah loved him and, just as I'd prayed for Rose for years before her adoption into their family, I'd prayed for Tom. I prayed that Sarah would grow up and be able to experience love, that she would be healthy, and live a life that she enjoyed. Tom was an answer to my prayers, just as Rose had been. He was a godly man who quickly fell deeply in love with Sarah. Just for that, I loved him too. The fact that he supported her decision to meet me and drove with her the three hours for this reunion made me appreciate him even more.

Sarah and I both loved the picture of us together, when she was six weeks old, at our last meeting. The day I held her up and she stopped crying because she knew my voice. We had also planned to perform a reenactment of that picture and made sure our outfits would match accordingly. Just like back then, so many years ago, I'd wear burgundy, and she'd wear pink. I'd sent her another copy of the picture, just to make sure. I looked at that photo again, while I waited for her, and marveled at how young we were. I realized that it was this very week, 27 years ago, that we'd unknowingly said our final goodbyes. Today, we would end that estrangement. No more distance in our relationship. Our lives would be forever reconnected; I knew it.

All of us waited outside for their arrival and, finally, our patience was rewarded. They were here! I bolted over to the driver's side door to hug my daughter, squeezing her as tightly as I dared. I barely even saw her face; I was so desperate to touch her, to confirm that this was happening, that she was real! She hugged me back, just as tightly. I was sure that I'd cry, but my eyes remained dry. She laughed and admitted that she thought I'd be sobbing too. The joy was so overwhelming that I didn't yet have tears for it. I knew they'd come eventually. The first couple of moments were a little awkward, but only a little.

She was so much more beautiful in person than I could have ever imagined! Even with the pictures I'd seen, none of them did her justice. Her nose, the tiny button I remembered, had grown but was still perfectly proportioned. Her porcelain skin and twinkling blue eyes shone at me, the same as in my memories. I wanted to stare, to watch her like I had when she was a newborn, but I didn't want to make her uncomfortable. I took a deep breath and forced myself to look away. I walked over to greet Tom and hugged him like the family he was. I told him how thankful I was that they'd come. Then, still struggling not to gawk at Sarah, I continued the introductions. Everyone already recognized each other from pictures, but I wanted to be polite. My husband Adam, and my other kids, Rachel, Lauren, and Mason. We all knew what a special day it was.

Mason, age six, had never been shy a day in his life. He quickly broke the ice and offered a tour of our house, gesturing grandly for Tom and Sarah to come inside. It was a little silly, but a perfect way to bring the couple into our life. Everything was certainly clean enough! We walked through the hallways, intermittently making small talk and giggling at Mason's showmanship. Adam and Tom were slightly more reserved; they knew how much Sarah and I had been looking forward to this day and weren't sure how things would unfold. Obviously, they hoped for the best, but they also wanted to be supportive if something went wrong. Sarah and I were unconcerned; we'd been bonding for nearly a year by that time. Mason dutifully led us through each room and then outside to show off our dog, Maddie. Completely out of character, Maddie immediately ran over to Sarah's legs, rolled onto her back, and then rubbed up against Sarah. She engaged with Sarah like they'd been long acquainted, like she recognized Sarah's smell and wanted to know where she'd been.

"Wow! She knows I'm family!"

Everyone was taken aback by the magnitude of it all, for a second, then we all burst out laughing at our crazy dog. Maddie had always been Rachel's dog. We expected a reaction like that when Rachel returned home from college, but never with anyone else. It was truly special and very fitting for the day. As we went back inside, still laughing about Maddie, I wanted to fill the space with words. I couldn't waste a single second being silent! I casually mentioned the ironic experience from the night before, when a couple named Lisa and James had been at the same Melodrama as me. I didn't mean anything by it; it was just another funny follow-up. Sarah paused and looked directly into my eyes.

"It was them."

I giggled briefly, thinking she was joking, but then I noticed the look on her face. I recognized that she was serious. I felt completely dumbfounded.

"Wait, what? Are you serious?"

The words didn't compute; she had to be joking. What were the chances that we'd end up there together, completely coincidentally? All of these years, I'd wondered if I was ever in the same place as them. I'd looked for Sarah in the eyes of so many strangers, looked for Lisa and James everywhere. Now, only hours before we'd finally reunite, there they were. In a tiny, local theater, nowhere near their home. And I'd had no idea. I couldn't believe it, then or now, three years later! Sarah explained that, earlier the day before, when I'd told her that I was headed for the Melodrama with some friends, she hadn't thought much about it. But, later, her mom had also texted her saying that they were going to the Melodrama. At first she didn't realize, but then she panicked. She hadn't told Lisa yet about her plan to meet me. She wanted to see how it went before facing that conversation.

At the time, I didn't know to what extent Sarah had confided in her parents about letting me be involved in her life. I didn't know what she wanted to share and what she wanted to hold back. It wasn't something we'd gotten around to discussing yet. The night previous, Sarah was the only one who knew both her parents and I would be in the same place at the same time. Who knew there was a possibility, however slim, that we could meet. Her adoptive parents and her birth mom, the birth mom she was planning to meet in person for the first time the next day. Had we met, I would have certainly mentioned their daughter's upcoming visit; it was all I could think about, after all! Sarah must have been so stressed. I could only imagine what she must have done, debating whether or not she should tell her mom or me.

She told me how she'd paced the floor, not knowing what the right decision was. Should she tell me to avoid making contact with them? To not mention our impending meet? What would I make of that kind of request? She had gotten to know me well, but it's impossible to predict every reaction. Or, she could confide in her mother, but it was her parents' anniversary. Who was she to ruin such a thing? Her parents worked hard and they deserved some time to themselves; time away from their worries. How would her mom react to the news? Would Lisa try to talk to me at the Melodrama or avoid me? Eventually, after turning over the myriad possibilities, Sarah decided to say nothing. Her decision ended up paying off because, despite my recognition of their names being called to celebrate their anniversary, I didn't recognize them. Our paths never crossed. The shock of that story made me question whether anything similar had ever happened before. Had we ever been so close in the past? Had I unknowingly walked right by them, maybe when they had Sarah with them, and somehow missed it?

After such a perfect icebreaker, we began talking up a storm. Hearing Sarah's voice, prettier and raspier than I had expected, was amazing. I loved watching her facial expressions and recognizing my own smile in hers. Lisa had been right about that. But that wasn't the only characteristic she'd inherited from me. We noticed that our bodies were built similarly, short and curvy, but petite. Spotting the comparisons, and the differences, was wild and exciting. As we sat around the table, I noticed that Adam was staring, a little longer than considered polite. I jokingly called it out, not wanting anyone to become uncomfortable.

"Hey, are you staring?"

Everyone laughed, no longer tense after the tour.

"It's kind of weird, you know. How much you look alike. Not even just your looks; you have the same mannerisms."

He gestured vaguely at us, trying to make his point. He wasn't wrong. I'd already been noticing how we paused on the same syllables and words for inflection, how we'd already begun finishing each other's sentences. At one point, when Adam had gotten up from the table and seen Sarah out of the corner of his eye, he'd mistaken her for me. He admitted that it was a little freaky. Tom sat quietly, for the most part. It hardly mattered—no one else could get a word in edgewise. Sarah and I talked nonstop, filling the air with stories and memories. Our bond only intensified in person; any worries I might have been harboring were long gone.

Lauren and Mason wandered off after some time, content to leave the adults and their boring anecdotes, and the rest of us went on our way to San Luis Obispo while Adam stayed behind to watch the kids. We wandered around aimlessly, with no real destination in mind. At one point, we stopped at Sephora. The three of us girls happily wandered the aisles while Tom waited outside. I didn't need anything. I was just so happy to spend the afternoon with my adult daughters. I came around a corner and saw Sarah, alone, contemplating an eyeshadow. It struck me then, how lovely she was, real and whole, intentionally spending her time with me. She glanced up at me and we smiled. It was our first encounter alone.

Afterwards, we headed to Firestone, a local restaurant I was familiar with and I knew we'd enjoy. As we sat there, Sarah told us how she and Tom had first met and how short their engagement had been before getting married. I hung on her every word, memorizing the details. I wanted to learn anything and everything I could about her life, whatever she was willing to share. As always, I ensured that she called the shots. I didn't want to overstep or do anything to jeopardize our budding relationship.

When we went to the soda machine, we grinned at our shared love of Coke and Pepsi. That was when Sarah told me that Lisa and James didn't know that she was visiting. She explained how she'd wanted to meet me first and see how things went. Of course, I respected her decision. She knew them best, after all. I told her how I'd always hoped I'd, one day, be able to reunite with them too.

After hours of enjoyment, we went back to my house. Rachel reminded us that we should take our reenactment picture and she agreed to be the photographer. For the next hour, the three of us worked hard to recreate the picture. Sarah practiced her baby face and I complained about my profile. Rachel instructed us to stand closer together, then to look more left or more right. We were all giggling and having fun. It was all a memory I'll never forget. We finally took that picture and many more besides. I never wanted the day to end.

While I was making dinner, I noticed Sarah reach over and grab an orange. She didn't ask for permission, and I loved that she knew she could. Nothing needed to be said; she felt comfortable and at home with us. My heart swelled at the idea. When I finished up, she had already started setting the table. She looked across the kitchen at me and laughed.

"I always wondered where I got my butt and now, I'm standing back here looking at it!"

I laughed too, knowing it was true. We all enjoyed mac and cheese with meatloaf. The food wasn't perfect, but no one minded. The night eventually grew late. Sarah didn't want to leave, and I completely agreed. However, she and Tom still had a three-hour drive home. It didn't seem to matter; we just kept talking. There was so much to share! Adam and Tom were more willing to add to the conversation, when they could, although Sarah and I continued to dominate it more often than not. Hours passed and, finally, we knew Sarah and Tom wouldn't get home until the wee hours of the morning. We hadn't even begun to scratch the surface, but, already, it felt perfect. The topic of her conception hadn't yet come up. As they prepared to leave, I stated very clearly to her:

"There is nothing I will not share with you; no question you cannot ask."

She smiled gently, knowing what I was offering. We knew another day would come; we had so much more to discover about each other. It didn't all need to happen today. On her way out, I heard her tell Tom,

"When we come back, next time, we'll plan to stay overnight."

Those words only reiterated what I already knew: there would be a next time. She'd had a good time with me. Tom seemed happy about the idea as well. As they drove away, with Tom driving the return trip, Sarah immediately started texting me. We talked about how much we'd enjoyed the outing and laughed about the events of the day. How Maddie had reacted, the look on my face when I'd discovered the Melodrama drama, recognizing our similarities, and the nature-versus-nurture argument as it related to the woman she'd become. I also pointed out her similarities to my other children. She and Rachel had a unique connection too. Despite those things, I recognized Lisa and James' loving nature, their compassionate personalities. The joy of the day filled my heart to the brim and spilled over as a love for life.

As I laid in bed that night, my mind ran over the day's events, again and again. It had been all I'd ever wanted. Seeing Sarah in my kitchen. Sitting together at my dining table, catching a glimpse of her in the back seat as we drove...she was simultaneously both strange and completely familiar. I loved watching her talk with Tom and engage with my kids, her siblings. The smallest things were important, from how she touched her face while she chatted, to how she threw her head back laughing. She had the same cowlick as me on the back of her head. We have that in common with my mom. Sarah could also thank her grandmother for the fair complexion, totally different from my olive skin tone, as well as her auburn hair. My mom used to have hair like that when she was young.

Replaying every moment, I stayed awake for their entire drive home. When they arrived, Sarah texted me a final "goodnight" along with a sincere commitment to seeing me again. That night, for the first time since I'd been a teenager, I slept all through the night. I didn't need the TV's background noise to distract me from anything.

As it turned out, I wouldn't have to wait very long for our next visit. Only two months later, Sarah and Tom came back again. We decided to go to an outdoor fair. Sarah bought a bag of popcorn that was nearly as tall as she was! At only 4'11, Sarah is only an inch shorter than me. As we walked along, toting the enormous popcorn and trying not to spill it everywhere, we encountered a street artist, asking if we wanted to do a caricature portrait. We all agreed it would be fun. Rachel and Sarah each took turns posing for the artist. I loved watching the two of them interact and get to know each other. The artist noticed our similarities and actually thought that we were all sisters! It seemed outrageous at the time, but, considering that Sarah is twenty years older than my youngest, Mason, me being sixteen years older than Sarah isn't so out of the question.

That night, we put on our pajamas and curled up on the couch with Oreos, Doritos, and soda, our collective favorites. I asked if Sarah wanted to know the story of her conception. I hurriedly explained that it wasn't a love story, or even remotely happy, but I would always be honest about it. I wasn't ashamed, but, with Tom by her side, I sure was nervous. I didn't want her to think less of me, but I especially didn't want her to think less of herself. She needed to know that, from the very beginning, she was loved. I never wanted her to doubt that. While I shared that story, from so long ago, all I saw was her compassion. She was neither broken nor destroyed by the impact of that tragedy. Instead, she was heartfelt and sympathetic.

"I am so sorry that happened to you."

I blinked back tears. She was only thinking of me. Time after time, I saw another example of God's faithfulness. Sarah was safe, not doubting her own worth or berating me. She had a solid foundation, parents who loved her, and a God she trusted. This tale did not shake her world or change who she was. She knew herself and didn't let the rape define her either. Something meant to destroy both of us, I suddenly realized, had no power. God's healing allowed us to hold fast and triumph.

After the visits started, it was clear that nothing would stand in the way of our blossoming, lifelong relationship. Initially, Sarah didn't share much about her illness and I didn't question her about it. It was her story to tell, whenever she felt comfortable. As far as I could see, appearance-wise, she looked perfectly healthy. There were no obvious symptoms, other than a brief, but persistent cough. Sarah was always able to physically keep up and, during my visits, I had not seen any significant impact on her life. Not to say that she wasn't fighting hard against an impossible challenge, but you'd never know it just from looking at her.

In the months that followed, we shared more than just occasional outings. We got together for family events too. Sarah made the trip up alone when Rachel graduated from college. It was so much fun to finally begin introducing Sarah to my extended family and friends. One of the crucial introductions was with my mom. I'd been telling her every detail of the visits since they began. I tried to put the emotions I felt, the deep healing, into words, to tell her just how precious Sarah was. I wasn't worried; I knew she'd love meeting Sarah too. What wasn't to love? I hoped, too, that finally reuniting with Sarah could bring my mom some healing as well.

My mom instantly recognized the family resemblances when they met again, and, more importantly, the beautiful heart shining through in Sarah. That connection warmed my soul. I'd been so excited to show Sarah the house I'd grown up in. The bedroom she'd once shared with me, in my womb. Introducing Sarah to my brother was equally special. I saw the joy in the way his eyes lit up at the sight of her. John had married his childhood sweetheart and they had four children of their own. He is a wonderful husband and father. He's always served God faithfully and raised his family in a loving home. They had moved to Washington just weeks before Mom's first stroke. The distance between all of us was even harder after our father's passing. Every visit was special. He had made the trip to see Rachel graduate and to meet Sarah, the niece he had thought of for a lifetime.

Sarah was in the kitchen, visiting with my brother and other members of the family. I sat in the living room, no longer needing to be involved in every moment with her, since now those moments happened on a regular basis. I heard my brother give a laugh from deep in his belly and announce that Sarah had just unknowingly given an exact performance of one of my well-known mannerisms. He couldn't get over how similar some of our behavior was. In that case, it was how she ran her fingers through her hair. Apparently, I do the same thing. It wasn't even something I'd previously been aware of. Sarah had told me that she instantly connected with her uncle, my brother. He reminded her of James, with his broad shoulders, shorter frame, as well as his chatty personality and gentle spirit.

That evening, as we both sat on the couch, next to each other, I looked down and had to smother a laugh. We both had our stubby legs extended towards the coffee table, crossed in the same direction, while we crossed our arms and slouched back into the cushions. It was hysterically ridiculous. She noticed me laughing and started in as well.

A few months later, Rachel had her 21st birthday. Sarah, Rachel, and I went on our first trip together, just us girls. We headed out to sunny Las Vegas. When Rachel and I arrived to pick Sarah up, she immediately jumped into the front seat, ahead of Rachel. It was such an instinctive reaction, one an older sister would do without thinking, and it delighted me. Rachel hardly minded; she'd grown up with two older brothers, so getting exiled to the backseat was a regular occurrence. The comfort level between us was higher than I could have hoped.

Despite that, I've always remained sensitive to Sarah's adoptive family. They will always be her primary family and her first priority. They should be! I never want Sarah to feel pulled in multiple directions or like she has to choose between us. I continue to honor the role I gave her parents years ago. That parenthood wasn't simply for her childhood; it's forever. Her sister, Rose, would always be her "sister". Neither Rachel nor Lauren would want to replace her. We all understood the dynamics and embraced our roles in her life. I am so grateful Sarah has welcomed me into her life. I am happy to share so many wonderful new experiences with her and make new memories, but I will never overstep my role in her life. I never want to assume. Sarah calls me Michelle, which feels right. I am not her mom, nor do I pretend to be. Ideally, I'd like for us to have a completely unique relationship, all our own. I hope that, one day, God-willing, I can reconnect with Lisa and James, and meet their other beautiful daughter, Rose. For now, I am thrilled to spend time with Sarah and Tom and will never be ungrateful for the gift that God has blessed me with.

Our trip to Las Vegas was so much fun! We stayed at a fantastic hotel with a relaxing lazy river. We spent hours there, floating around and admiring the palm trees. We shared stories and people-watched, another past time we all enjoyed. For dinner, we went to a Mexican restaurant to celebrate Rachel's birthday, advising the waiter of our occasion. When the waiter arrived, he instantly asked how we were related since we all looked so similar. We giggled, reveling in the moment. For someone unfamiliar with our story to recognize us as family was a wonderful experience. I soaked it in, loving every moment.

On the flight home, Sarah began to open up more about her life with cystic fibrosis. She talked about her childhood hospitalizations and her parents' love and prayers. She was especially excited about a new CF drug that was starting clinical trials. Apparently, it had demonstrated enough to make researchers optimistic about slowing down or stopping symptoms altogether. It still had a year or more to go in testing, but the possibilities it offered were enticing. I was thrilled to hear about a miracle drug, and I cherished the hope it gave. The health, the quality of life, and the years it might add to Sarah's life.

Additionally, she confided in me even more about how eager she was to become pregnant. She wants so badly to become a mom. I encouraged her, saying that God had given her that wish. He would fulfill her heart's desires. I was confident that she would have the opportunity to experience pregnancy and motherhood. I was honored that she felt comfortable enough to share all of these things with me.

Over the years, I had lost contact with my friend, Kim. She'd been the one to tell me of God's promise for my reunion with Sarah. However, now that Sarah and I had reconnected, I had to try and find Kim again. I was anxious to tell her God's faithfulness, the story of seeing the tulips, and how Sarah had reached out to me the next day. Kim was happy to hear from me again. She felt blessed that God had used her to deliver such an important message of hope so many years before. We stayed in touch after that. She often asked about Sarah and her health, but was confident that God has sustained her life and would continue to do so.

In January of 2018, I shared with Kim how Sarah had become depressed about not being able to have children yet. That she had been trying for some time and was discouraged, losing hope. Kim was very direct about what she felt God wanted me to know and gave me a new promise from Him, again offering a light for a future that had yet to unfold.

"Sarah will have children. It will happen. July is the month of breakthrough; she shall live and be fruitful. July! July! July! It shall rain blessings in July. She had been told she will not have children and that is a lie! Every mind-binding spirit, those things rehearsing in her mind that people have told her; they are not the truth, nor aligned with the Word of God…"

I was thrilled to share this with Sarah! She knew that God could speak through others to impart truth and His promises. We both held onto this promise of hope through the years that followed.

When Sarah and Tom bought their first house, I was very excited to visit. I couldn't wait! Up until then, I'd been eager to have them meet all of my friends and family, but hadn't been invited to be involved in their world. I quietly looked forward to that day, and it seemed like it was finally time. This would be a first step. I went alone, not wanting to be too invasive with my large, outgoing family. As I drove there, the magnitude of the opportunity dawned on me for the upteenth time. I smiled to myself, gripping the steering wheel a little tighter. Sarah's home was the most personal space she could offer me. Once I'd admired the home, as with before, we sat and talked for hours. Tom faithfully joined us, content to mostly listen. Tom and I had quickly connected, ever since the first visit. Our conversations had been easy, though he wasn't as talkative as his wife. He is the same age as my older boys and I easily assumed maternal feelings for him.

The second night of my stay at their house, Tom asked if I would be comfortable having his parents, Thomas and Jodi, come over. I was thrilled at the offer. Finally, a chance to meet the people in their life! I insisted, of course they should come! I had been looking forward to the opportunity for some time. I certainly wanted to meet Lisa and James too, but I didn't want to push my luck. I went upstairs to freshen up and, before long, I heard unfamiliar voices down below. I headed back downstairs to introduce myself and excitedly embrace my growing family. Tom's parents had also brought one of his sisters along, Carly. I hurried down the stairs.

"Hello!"

The looks on their faces were priceless; it was clear how much I reminded them of Sarah. Thomas laughed.

"Oh, wow! I thought you were Sarah!"

"Yeah, the similarities are amazing!"

It was fun to meet them. They were really interested in our story and listened attentively. Just as my husband had been caught staring at Sarah, fascinated with how much we looked alike, so they stared at me that evening.

242

I was so proud Tom had wanted me to meet his family. Jodi, Carly, Sarah, and I spent hours chatting while the men sat in the living room, watching football. Jodi, confided that Tom had told her when I'd first met with Sarah and the plans leading up to it. She'd warned him to be very careful and to watch out for Sarah. In her experience, she'd heard of birth moms who were only after money, and she didn't want them to go in unwary of my possible intentions. That night, she laughed at how far-fetched those ideas were. I laughed along, but I knew her attitude was necessary. I remembered many birth moms I had dealt with in my time with Child Protective Services, especially the cases where I'd had to remove their children. I would have felt the same way.

On my second visit to Tom and Sarah's house, I brought Mason and Lauren with me. That time, we were all invited to Thomas and Jodi's house where I was also able to meet Tom's other sister, Whitney. I loved the fact that they really saw me as part of the family and as a mom. My children are my world. I had been a mom, then, for more than 27 years. They recognized that and welcomed me eagerly into their lives. Jodi showed me pictures of her kids throughout the years. It was fun to see Tom as a baby. I replied that I couldn't wait until Sarah and Tom have kids themselves and we both smiled at the thought.

In an example of what had become our new normal, Sarah and Tom joined us when we went to celebrate Daniel as he graduated from Teen Challenge. Typically a one year program, it had now been five years since his first brush with death. This time, not only did he graduate, but he found his passion again in music. With his whole family occupying the entire first row, along with our dear friends, Mike, Jennifer and Michaela, we watched proudly as he led the service through worship, each of us recognizing God's amazing healing in his life. He was then to begin the next phase of his journey at Teen Challenge Ministry Institute. We were all so proud of him, me most of all. I knew how hard he had worked at this, had seen firsthand the initial days of deciding to get clean, the many times he had to stop and restart. We didn't know it then, but, during the next two years in the ministry program, his life would change forever. He'd meet the woman who would become his wife, Khrystina Elizabeth. I could not be happier for him.

After two years of trading visits back and forth between Sarah's house and mine, I received an unexpected gift that I truly cherished. At the end of another girls-only weekend with Rachel and Sarah, we went to drop off Sarah at her church. They were planning a family night, complete with dinner, snacks, and volleyball. Tom was already there and Sarah wanted me to meet her friends. If she was excited for it, I certainly was too! The second we arrived, Sarah immediately began introducing me to one person after another, in rapid succession. I would have been fine if she'd just called me Michelle, without any further explanation. Rachel and I had not planned to meet anyone who knew our whole story. But, as we moved around the area, Sarah beamed with pride, telling each person that I was her birth mom, Michelle, with her daughter, Rachel.

Sarah wasn't embarrassed or ashamed at all. I didn't know that there were any more levels of healing that I could achieve, but, in that moment, I felt beyond blessed. I was shocked, for one thing, that she was comfortable enough to do that. I followed after her bubbly energy, trying not to look like I was in a blissed-out stupor. She began to introduce me to another family, but hardly got out two words before they interrupted her, saying I needed no introduction, it was obvious! We all laughed together, no awkwardness at all.

When Rachel and I finally said our goodbyes and climbed into the car, my heart overflowed with joy. I told Rachel that I'd just experienced my lifelong dream unfold right in front of me. I had always tried to live a life that Sarah could be proud of and, in this moment, for the first time since we had reconnected, I didn't doubt that pride for a second. My prayers for decades had truly been answered.

In September of 2019, Sarah and I had been planning a trip, just the two of us. We were flying to Arizona to meet with a publisher to discuss my book and our story. I was elated to have several days alone with Sarah, for us to spend time together. We had probably said all we could ever think to say in our years of being reconnected, but this was a first for us. I was excited, not even a little nervous. We were scheduled to fly out of Burbank airport and I'd pick up Sarah on my way there. Two days before we were meant to leave, she texted me something I'd never anticipated. She had told Lisa and James about our trip and the reason for our adventure. Her parents were happy to hear about the plan and invited Sarah to bring me by their office on our way to the airport.

Sarah wanted to know if I'd be okay with that. Of course I was! All these years later, they were finally ready to see me again. My answer has been, and will always be, yes. Although, I checked in with her, to see if she was ready for that. She agreed that she was. She knew it should happen. After all, our lives are completely connected in all ways. This was the last step. That's when the nerves began to creep in. They still didn't know my side of the story; how would I tell them a lifetime of information in the few moments we'd have in the visit? I hoped that they could see my heart and would love me. I had no hard feelings towards them, despite the years of silence. It didn't matter that I didn't understand; I was honored to reunite with them and maintained my respect for them. I trusted that God's timing would be perfect, the way it had been so many times before.

When the day arrived, I spent extra time getting ready, just as I had when I met them for the first time, nearly thirty years before. I still wanted to make a good impression. I chose a red, flowing sundress. Red was always a good choice with the combination of my skin tone and dark hair. My bags were packed and excitement filled the air. Here I was, meeting with a publisher to discuss my story, our story. Now, I was driving to reunite with Lisa and James, just hours before I'd fly out. Everything seemed surreal. I was about an hour away from Sarah's when I received a text from the airline. Our flight had been cancelled.

What? No way! What would we do? It was possible to drive to Arizona, I quickly reasoned, but we needed to investigate a little. I called Sarah and she agreed to look into options while I continued driving the rest of the way to her place. A little while later, she called back with good news and bad news. The good news: we could jump onto a different flight; the bad news: it wouldn't allow us enough time to meet up with her parents. Although I was disappointed, we both agreed to catch the earlier flight. We accepted that today was not the day God had planned for the reunion. However, now I knew that Lisa and James did want to see me again, so I still felt that my prayers had been, in some way, answered.

# EPILOGUE

*"So shall My word be that goes forth from My mouth; It shall not return to Me void, But it shall accomplish what I please, And it shall prosper in the thing for which I sent it." (Isaiah 55:11)*

July, 2020. It has been more than four years since Sarah and I began this journey together to reconnect. We have continued to build our unique relationship, one of love and respect for the life the other has lived. The life we now share. We innately love each other's family and the role they all play in both of our lives. Our hearts are big enough to include them all. I no longer feel like I have to be careful with my words; she knows me well enough to understand. She gives me the benefit of the doubt when I need it, and I do the same for her. We text daily and visit each other often. Once, I didn't allow myself to hope for such a close relationship, but now we share more than I ever could have fathomed. Now, I let myself dream of our future, safe in the knowledge that it'll be intertwined.

If only I had known how perfect life would eventually be, I might have taken refuge in that, during the years of heartache and pain. But, whenever I think that, God gently reminds me that, many years ago, He gave me a promise through my friend, Kim. When the tulips bloom, you will be reunited with your daughter. Yes, it was vague, and it didn't give much in the way of a time frame, but it did offer hope. Had I held onto that promise, as God had intended, the years of silence and broken promises would not have had the same impact; I wouldn't have been robbed of my joy. I could have lived, peacefully, while I waited for God's faithfulness. I'd know that a reunion was already destined to happen. Yet, in the midst of everyday life, it is hard to remember that God's timing is not our timing, and His plans are not ours. When I hear God's voice now, I try to do better. To trust that God is in control.

In late January, Sarah was approved for the new miracle drug marketing for cystic fibrosis. We hoped that it would provide Sarah with improved quality of life and, in the six months that have followed, she feels amazing. Her lung capacity is greater, she has more energy, and her cough has been rendered nearly non-existent. We are all so thankful for the medical advances over the years. They have sustained Sarah's life, with God's help. As I continue to pray for her health, I am grateful for where she is now and the beautiful future she's been promised.

With Sarah's struggle, over the past four years, to become pregnant, I have held onto God's promise that she will have children. Each month, we go through the same cycle: period, ovulation, anticipation, and disappointment as another period arrives. I have tried to stay strong for her, knowing that this is her journey to trust God and His promise. I empathize with her pain; I know how hard it is waiting, not knowing, and not even wanting to dream too much for fear of crushing disappointment. I remind her of God's promise. I know she trusts Him, but it can be difficult to hold on to faith.

I still hope. I pray that, one day, I might have a relationship with Lisa and James; that we could embrace each other, and acknowledge our jobs as well done. That our love for each other, and for Sarah, can help us look past the years of misinformation and the adoption agency's lies. I hope to eventually meet Rose, the sister that God gave Sarah, now a woman herself. I have prayed for her journey, too.

I have been writing this book for two years now. Concluding it has been difficult, as I have continued to live out this epilogue in real time. It was supposed to be completed September of 2019 and, if it had, this is where it would have ended; God had another plan.

July 21, 2020. I was driving to Starbucks, on my way to work, when Sarah called me. I saw her contact name, "New Joy Sarah," pop up on my phone and, somehow, I knew the message would be important. We mostly text; phone calls are pretty rare between us. I also knew what day it was; I tracked Sarah's cycles as much as she did, using an app on my phone. She should have started her period on Sunday; it was now Tuesday. I'd texted her over the weekend to see how she was doing, but she hadn't said anything specific, and I didn't push. It had now been three days and I hadn't held her hand through another month of disappointment.

She casually greeted me with a moment of small talk. I could hardly concentrate, my own heart in my throat. Then she hung up, saying she'd call me back soon, but Tom was calling her right then. I arrived at Starbucks, my hands sweating and my mind racing. I wasn't able to pick up my drink before she called back and I fumbled for a second with the phone, adrenaline coursing through my veins. Anticipation sat heavy on my tongue, but I remained cautious.

"Well, I guess your friend was right about July."

Her tone was even, like the words meant nothing special, but we both knew the truth. God's promise had been fulfilled! Overwhelmed with God's love and my complete joy, I began crying and laughing simultaneously. She sounded similarly choked up on the other side of the line and reiterated her own overwhelming joy:

"Yeah, I am pregnant!"

# SARAH'S AFTERWORD

It was early 1997, I was seven years old, and my parents moved us to a new house. It was much more spacious than our previous house and right down the street from my Grandpa. We had a few dogs and I attended private school. Life was idyllic. I couldn't have asked for more. However, I'd soon receive more because, unbeknownst to me, my parents had been pursuing another adoption through the same agency they'd used to find me.

After a couple of months in our new house, they were matched with another baby girl. I was really excited at the prospect of having a little sister, who they told me would be named Rose. I recall my parents coming into my room, sitting me down on a Friday evening, and telling me that, soon, I would be a big sister. We had to wait until Monday to meet her and that seemed like an eternity to my mind! I spent the entire weekend tidying my room and making it ready for the baby. I was sorely disappointed when I found out from my mom that Rose would be sleeping in a bassinet in their room for a while. She wouldn't get to share my room right away, even though I'd spent all that time cleaning and preparing it! I'm sure I pouted obnoxiously at the news.

Monday finally came; Rose was nine days old. Mom and I wore matching long, flowy, pink gingham dresses. I wanted to look especially fancy and older, like I was ready to take on the responsibilities of being a big sister. I'd seen TV and heard people talk at school about babies and having siblings; I knew that, as the eldest, I would have to help Mom and be more grown up. I couldn't be the baby anymore.

When we arrived, I sat on the brown couch between my parents. The social worker came in, followed by the foster mom who held my little sister. My parents both began to cry, a response I didn't understand at the time. This was such a happy occasion! Why were they crying? I patted my mom awkwardly, not sure how to react to them, but was quickly distracted by the foster mom placing Rose very gently into my arms. She guided my hands and showed me how to cradle the baby's head properly. Rose nestled into my chest. I noticed that she was also wearing a pink gingham dress and I was incredibly pleased. My second thought was that her little legs were the same size, shape, and color as raw Italian sausage links. That seemed...kind of freaky to me, but I accepted it, nonetheless.

That's not a comparison most young children would draw, but, in my family, we had a tradition of making our own sausage links. My Grandpa and Dad would hand make a few hundred pounds of sausages a couple of times a year. My Grandpa was a first-generation Italian-American, with his family originally Sicilian. His mom came through Ellis Island while she was pregnant with him in the early 1920s. We kept the family tradition alive and well, which is how I knew, even then, what raw sausages looked like.

During the car ride home from the adoption agency, I sat right beside Rose, just staring at her. She started crying at one point, and I rushed to try and console her. However, she cried so hard that she gave herself the hiccups and kept interrupting her own cries by hiccupping. Eventually, it made her leave off the crying when she couldn't control it any longer. I giggled, thinking it was the funniest thing.

I had been an only child for my whole life, so it was a big adjustment for me to learn to share my parents' time and attention, no matter what promises I'd made about being more grown up. Bringing home Rose changed my life forever in many ways, but I'll always treasure it because it gave me a best friend.

\*\*\*\*\*\*\*\*\*\*\*\*\*\*\*\*\*\*\*\*\*\*\*\*\*\*\*\*\*\*\*\*\*\*\*\*\*\*\*\*\*\*\*\*\*\*\*\*\*\*\*\*\*\*\*\*\*\*\*

Growing up with a terminal disease meant nothing to me when I was young. I didn't understand the circumstances of my condition or how it would impact my life. I was, otherwise, a perfectly normal child. Since I was diagnosed at eighteen months of age, I never knew any other life. Breathing treatments in the morning and evening were just standard. Having to stop by the school office to get my medication before lunch and recess was part of the daily routine. I figured that laying inverted, on an inclined workout bench, while my mom used chest compression therapy, watching Sesame Street upside down, was the norm for all five-year-olds.

In hindsight, I can see that I was forced to mature at a young age. I had to quickly learn to swallow ludicrously large pills, know to wake up early on school days to get my treatments done, and gain a basic understanding of macronutrients long before I could pronounce the words properly. I had to know which foods required special digestive enzymes, such as ice cream or a hamburger, and which ones didn't, like popsicles and pretzels.

Despite my hardships, I knew that it was especially difficult for my parents. No one is meant to bury their children. With my prognosis, I was unlikely to even see my teen years. Like all parents, they didn't feel adequately prepared to raise a child with special needs. However, they knew that God had not let them wait nine years to fulfill their dreams of parenthood only for things to end like that. They might not have known how long I had, but they were determined to do all they could to keep me healthy. With support from their church, they dove headfirst into research on cystic fibrosis. They read every book on the topic, attended every convention they could access, and fundraised every year. My father worked hard to ensure that I had the best health insurance that money could buy. To this day, my mom is my strongest advocate when I need assistance navigating the red tape of doctors and other healthcare professionals.

All things considered, I remained relatively healthy. Around the age of seven, my mom developed carpal tunnel syndrome, and it became increasingly difficult for her to perform the chest compression therapy. Of course, I didn't know how much pain she was in as she faithfully continued, despite the pain. However, due to those extenuating circumstances, we were able to acquire a machine called The Vest. It was cutting-edge technology at the time and very expensive. As the name suggested, it was a vest that connected with hoses and used air to mimic the compression effects of the chest therapy. It's a machine I still use to this day.

Around nine, I was hospitalized for the first time. Every nurse in the pediatric department was surprised that I hadn't needed hospitalization before then, but my parents still felt responsible, like they had failed me in some way. During the stay, my doctor suggested that I should be enrolled in local swimming classes. Apparently, they would do wonders for my lung capacity. In fact, I enjoyed swimming so much that I began doing synchronized swimming competitively with the City of Los Angeles from then until I was sixteen. I wasn't hospitalized again until after I stopped competing, but then there were a string of hospital stays and lengthy bouts on IV antibiotics.

When I was seventeen, my health had been on a steady downward spiral. I'd been hospitalized a few times that year, and the sadness had begun to weigh heavily on me. The nurse at my cystic fibrosis clinic told me that I would qualify for the Make-A-Wish Foundation, if I wanted, but that I should do it soon because it is only available for people under eighteen. My parents were skeptical about it; I wasn't dying. Not like the kids in the commercials, small, fragile waifs in wheelchairs with no hair.

Despite their reservations, they allowed me to put in an application and some people from the foundation came to interview me. One person took me aside and asked what I wanted. I didn't really know how the process worked, but I told her that I wanted to go to Europe. I think I named Paris first, because I recall listing all the countries in Western Europe since I wasn't picky. When we went back into the room to join everyone else, the foundation worker immediately told my parents I'd said I wanted to go to Paris. My mom gave me a disapproving look, disappointed that I'd made such an outlandish request. The other foundation worker commented that Make-A-Wish had never fulfilled any international wishes before. My parents quickly assured them that it wasn't necessary, but the worker made it clear that just because it hadn't been done didn't mean it couldn't be done.

They left and a few weeks went by before we received a call. Make-A-Wish had found a sponsor for me; a fashion designer who'd heard I wanted to go to Paris and wanted to fund the whole trip. My whole family could come too. All four of us would be going to Paris for a week! The local news channel came to my house to report on it. A cameraman spent the whole day talking to me and getting some B-roll footage leading up to the evening when we went to an outdoor shopping center in Los Angeles. It was around Christmastime, so the center was outfitted for the festivities. There was a crowd and multiple cameras, all filming me.

I met my sponsor and he gave me $500 for a shopping spree in his store, along with two suitcases to take on my trip. It was a high-end

255

boutique store, so the money only could afford about three items, but the entire experience was totally insane. I was so excited! Coming out of the dressing room, modeling expensive clothing in front of strangers and camera crews was an unforgettable time. The story made the ten o'clock news that night, and my city put it on the front cover of our newspaper that month. It was like a Cinderella fairytale story.

Once I turned eighteen, I transitioned into the adult CF care team. We had had a very strong relationship with my pediatric care team, and everyone was so supportive. That was no longer the case with the new team. The doctors didn't appreciate anything that they interpreted as questioning their methods, which included asking about treatment plans we'd done independent research on. They were very adamant that I needed to come to appointments alone, without my mom the way I always had. As a teen, it was very intimidating to have multiple doctors and social workers in my exam room forcing my mom to leave.

It was wildly inappropriate and a complete abuse of power. They didn't have the ability to forbid my mom from being present; I was already a legal adult. I could consent to having a family member in the room. Those few months of fighting with the CF adult team made us realize that they had their own agenda and weren't looking out for my best interests. It all came to a head when I was hospitalized at nineteen. I'd been a patient for over a week and wasn't getting any better. The CF care team came to my room, shrugged, and told me that there was nothing more they could do for me. They told me to get my affairs in order.

I was horrified! I was still a teenager and my parents were absolutely devastated. We all knew I was sick, but I hadn't seemed that sick. After several very emotional hours, the routine resident doing rounds came by my room to examine me. He flipped through my charts and wondered why they hadn't administered a different drug.

"Huh. Why haven't they tried that with you yet? I'm going to ask…"

Four days later, I was discharged from the hospital. I was given two weeks of the medication he had recommended and was able to go home, finally on the mend. I left the hospital grateful for God's mercy, but very aware that we needed to find a different CF care team. This one wasn't going to work. My mom did some research and, luckily, found my current doctor. It's an hour plane ride away, but the change in quality is well worth it.

\*\*\*\*\*\*\*\*\*\*\*\*\*\*\*\*\*\*\*\*\*\*\*\*\*\*\*\*\*\*\*\*\*\*\*\*\*\*\*\*\*\*\*\*\*\*\*\*\*\*\*\*\*\*\*\*\*\*\*\*\*\*\*

I don't recall exactly when I found out that I had been adopted. It's a question I'm frequently asked. I guess I've always known. We had several storybooks on the topic, and my parents would often tell me about adoption and what it meant. I always grew up knowing that I had a birth mom and that she loved me so much that she wanted me to have parents who also loved me and could raise me. I never felt abandoned or questioned my birth mom's motives, though I've come to learn that is quite common for adopted children. Usually, I'm asked one of two questions, both of which I've grown to hate:

"Have you ever met your real mom?" or "Why did she give you up?"

I didn't resent people for asking, but they began to grate early on. James and Lisa are my real parents. There's no denying it, and I'd often respond in kind. They're the ones God chose to parent me, so they're my parents. What the asker meant was "birth mom." I knew that, but I couldn't help my obnoxious retort because I hated the implication that Lisa wasn't my real mom. As for the other query, telling people that Michelle was only sixteen when I was born was enough of an answer.

I always knew that I eventually wanted to meet my birth mom, but for whatever reason—fears, family loyalty, worry that it might disrupt my life too much—I had little interest in meeting her as a kid or teen. I promised myself that I'd reach out when I was engaged to be married. I don't know why I chose that marker of adulthood, just that I wanted Michelle to be at my wedding. My mom had married my dad at eighteen, so I assumed it would also happen with me at a relatively young age as well. I didn't get engaged until I was 24, as it turned out. However, with all of the change happening in my life at that time, I forgot about the decision to contact Michelle until eight months after I'd been married.

\*\*\*\*\*\*\*\*\*\*\*\*\*\*\*\*\*\*\*\*\*\*\*\*\*\*\*\*\*\*\*\*\*\*\*\*\*\*\*\*\*\*\*\*\*\*\*\*\*\*\*\*\*\*\*\*\*\*\*\*\*\*\*\*

It was late 2014, and I worked for my parents. There was another girl, Katie, who also worked there as a receptionist. She always came in an hour before me. On one particular day, she had been working on a project: cleaning out boxes of paperwork. I walked over to my desk and, on the keyboard, was a graduation announcement of someone who looked a lot like me. I was one semester from finishing college myself, so cap and gown photo shoots were already on my mind. I was perplexed at the picture, but Katie interrupted my confused musings.

"That must be your birth mom! She looks just like you!"

Oh! Right! Of course it was! I should have known right away. But, at eight in the morning on a work day, it wasn't a place where I expected to see her. Katie started in on questions about my adoption and my birth mom, but she quickly realized that I didn't have very many answers. I certainly didn't know what my birth mom was up to now. That conversation got me thinking: I ought to reach out to Michelle. Why not? I was an adult, a married woman, in fact. I was almost done with school. A lot had happened in my life and, I knew, instinctively, that it was time.

When I told her about my thoughts, Katie was vehement that I shouldn't make a hasty decision after only seeing a photo. As my parents' employee, she was loyal and didn't want me to do something that could potentially hurt them. It didn't turn out to be a hasty decision, but it was a definitive one. I hadn't given the matter much thought at all, but, suddenly seeing that photograph after nothing for years; I knew instantly that reconnecting was what I needed to do.

I spoke to my husband, Tom, about it over the next few weeks. He was remarkably hesitant about it, since he'd had some friends who'd also been adopted and their experiences reaching out to their birth moms hadn't gone well, but he was always very supportive of me and my choices. I began to compose a message to send over Facebook. It wasn't too long, just a brief update on current events in my life and a few photos.

With every fiber of my being, I knew that Michelle would absolutely respond and be very receptive to a relationship with me. I told Tom, when I push "Send," our life changes forever. I knew there was no going back after that. He understood my decision, though privately, he still held some reservations. I clicked "Send." It was done. I resigned myself to wait.

A few hours went by, no response. Then a few days went by, still no response. That was strange. Maybe my mom had over-exaggerated how much Michelle wanted to be involved in my life? After a few more days, I resent the message, thinking somehow it didn't go through properly. A week later, I felt insecure about the entire thing. Maybe she had moved on and didn't want to be reminded of her past. I knew she had several more children now. My parents must have been mistaken about her. She wasn't interested in getting to know me after all. It was with a heavy heart that I let the matter go. I couldn't know then that she had never received my message.

Several months went by and I received a social media follow request from Rachel, who I knew was Michelle's daughter. Excitement flowed through me once more. It wouldn't be long before I saw pictures of Rachel, Michelle, and the rest of their family. A few short weeks later, Michelle and I would finally connect.

\*\*\*\*\*\*\*\*\*\*\*\*\*\*\*\*\*\*\*\*\*\*\*\*\*\*\*\*\*\*\*\*\*\*\*\*\*\*\*\*\*\*\*\*\*\*\*\*\*\*\*\*\*\*\*\*\*\*\*\*

However, as much as I have loved connecting with Michelle, it is often difficult to put my feelings into words. Since day two of my life, Lisa has been my mom, in every sense of the word, physically, emotionally, spiritually, and legally. Nothing will ever change that. No one could possibly alter my love for my parents and the role they play in my life. I have a keen sense of family and loyalty to our name, heritage, and the identity I was raised with.

While I bore Michelle no malice or ill-will, I had little desire to meet her before 2015. I was content in the life I led. I had no burning questions or feelings of emptiness when I thought about that aspect of my past. However, once I had decided to throw myself headlong into this journey, it has filled voids within me I never knew existed. Meeting her provided pieces of a puzzle I hadn't known were missing. A lot of it was in the little things. Seeing the strong familial resemblance in our appearances and mannerisms, approaching a topic in the same, analytic way, and finding that, not only do we have the same sense of humor, but we even laugh in the same way!

Having said all of that, I am profoundly aware of Michelle's presence in my life. She fulfills a maternal role and is a dear friend. And, yet, she is neither. There is no good word to encompass what she means to me. We stepped into a mother-child relationship as two adults, both of us married, within our own growing households. In many ways, I think by not knowing Michelle in my youth, I was better able to participate in our relationship now.

I take comfort in knowing I can talk to Michelle about anything. I don't have that level of comfort with anyone else. It's a unique situation; there's the inherent knowledge of Michelle's unconditional, maternal love that provides a safety net in sharing my thoughts and feelings. We have formed a deep friendship, due in part to our myriad of similarities. When I talk to her, it feels like I'm speaking with someone who's known me my whole life.

# ABOUT THE AUTHOR

Michelle Lee Graham is a dynamic, inspirational mother and leader. Her vulnerability, honesty, and authenticity help deliver a multifaceted motivational message. Michelle has faced trauma, tragedy, and loss, but has been able to discover great love, relationships, and success. She strives to beat the odds and not let others define her.

At the young age of sixteen, Michelle was the survivor of a violent sexual assault. Though the impact of the rape did not define her, the ensuing pregnancy most definitely did! Michelle had her first child at sixteen. Through adoption, Michelle was able to express her unselfish love and give her daughter the life she deserved. Moving forward would mean living a life that her daughter, Sarah, could be proud of.

As a Chief Executive Officer (CEO) for more than a decade, Michelle has built a successful career as an empathetic leader with a high emotional intelligence. Her professionalism and integrity have helped build a successful organization; navigating her team through significant restructure, growth, and success!

Michelle went on to have five more children of her own. Through many good, and bad, life choices, she has lived a life full of passion, vulnerability, professionalism and success. She believes that we all have the possibility to experience the freedom to truly Love, Forgive, Grow, Heal and find New Joy! Sometimes, we just need a little help to get there. It is Michelle's desire to train, coach and inspire others to discover their New Joy.

# OPPORTUNITIES FOR YOU

As an inspirational author, trainer, coach, motivational speaker, and leader, Michelle Lee Graham wants the opportunity to support you!

### BONUS 1 "#Undefined by Rape" Facebook Group

Michelle created the group "Undefined by Rape" as a place for survivors of sexual abuse to come and find a network of friends and personal healing. Within this group, you will find supportive, authentic people who are willing to be vulnerable and kind.

### BONUS 2: One-On-One Coaching With Michelle

Pregnancy, parenting, marriage, aging, and life as a whole didn't come with a handbook. Fortunately for us, we have each other. Michelle has experienced a lot of life, from teen pregnancy, adoption, single parenting, marriage, divorce, re-marriage, the death of a parent, to tremendous personal and professional success. Through it all, she has learned to unlock her own motivation and strength. Let her help you do the same!

### BONUS 3: Motivational Speaker and Trainer

Unlock your power, healing, love, passion, joy, forgiveness, inspiration, and success!

Michelle Lee Graham has been inspiring and motivating others for many years. As the CEO of a large non-profit and a mother of five, Michelle has still found time to be an author, educator, coach, and mentor. Michelle brings an engaging and dynamic presentation that always motivates and empowers those around her.

Through humor, straight talk, and putting it all on the table, Michelle has the ability to relate to any audience. This includes managers, leaders, parents, teens, and anyone who needs to find their passion.

MICHELLELEEGRAHAM.COM